THE
RAPTURED

A CATHOLIC VIEW OF THE
LATTER DAYS
AND THE SECOND COMING

John W. Tombler

and

Hubert J. Funk

Trumpet Press, Inc.

East Orange, N.J.

Copyright © 1977 by Trumpet Press, Inc., East Orange, N.J.

ISBN 0-918952-01-8

Library of Congress Catalog Card No.: 77-8-0110

We are pleased to dedicate this Volume
to
"our 'old' scripture prof,"
Bishop John J. Dougherty,
who first unveiled for us
the mysteries
of the
Prophetic Word

Contents

Appendices

Foreword

Since La Salette and Fatima, much interest has been aroused in the subject of the latter days and the Second Coming of Christ. Numerous private revelations are claimed purporting to foretell the end-time events, all of them claiming that they will be soon. These statements and claims have to be checked against official Church teaching and the Scriptures, according to Benedict XIV. Unfortunately, there is no official teaching on this subject yet, and while a good part of Scripture deals with the events of the last years of this era, it is not arranged systematically, leading to much confusion. Earlier attempts at presenting this in an orderly fashion were hopelessly complicated by the fact that there is a natural tendency to see everything in light of one's own era, and since the events were still distant, the conclusions drawn were vitiated.

Between A.D. 1200 and A.D. 1600 numerous apocalyptic movements formed, at a time when the Moslems threatened Europe, the papacy was split, famine and plagues raged through Europe. Napoleon's era produced similar excitement. In our era of world wars, hydrogen bombs and other "doomsday" weapons, the same fears are spreading again. This is particularly true since the foundation of the state of Israel. It is important, therefore, to have a clear exposition of what God has foretold, in order to see things in perspective. That way emotional claims of fanatics may be allayed and a reasonable view maintained.

Since we are dealing with God's revelation and a part of the deposit of faith, knowledge of this should be spread, even preached. This is what the apostles did, and it should be done in our times also. There is no reason for neglecting a part of our religion. The apparent obscurity of the subject can be overcome by a systematic, comprehensive treatment of the subject. It is not possible yet to get a definitive treatment of the subject. That can only occur when the events themselves are imminent and at the door. Meanwhile, we are presenting a tentative outline which hopefully will be corrected and improved as the future brings clearer insights.

J. W. T.
H. J. F.

THE RAPTURED

A CATHOLIC VIEW OF THE
LATTER DAYS
AND THE SECOND COMING

I

Part I

The Future in a Teacup

The Lord IS Coming!

For some reason or other those words frighten me. I do not know why. I love the Lord. I love the Lord in mind and heart and soul. I want to be with Him. I am not afraid to admit that I am tempted to stray from Him on sundry and varied occasions. Temptations abound. Nevertheless, I am certain, I simply know, I love the Lord. I delight in His presence. Why, then, do I feel afraid when I hear the words "The Lord is coming"?

A certain shrinking sensation, a tensing of the body, of the stomach muscles occurs. This, I think, is a strange reaction. Yet I sense that it is a rather typical reaction. I think it is, perhaps, the initial reaction we experience when we learn that we are going to meet someone upon whom we wish to make a good impression face to face for the first time. Am I worthy to meet the Lord? Will He accept me as one of His company? Will He, indeed, love me? These are the thoughts which pass through my mind when I hear those words. My faults, failures, sins flash before me and I cringe in horror.

Yet at the same time I am aware that the Lord does love me, is with me, dwells within me. Such contradictory emotions within me arouse feelings of longing and a nervous anticipation, feelings of hope and despair at one and the same moment and an intense desire that the Lord come quickly, thus resolving the emotional conflicts.

An engaged couple, for example, usually know each other reasonably well. Nevertheless, as the actual time of the marriage approaches they frequently enough experience a nervous anxiety, feelings of doubt and uncertainty. Looking forward to the coming of the Lord, the feelings, I suspect, are somewhat the same.

1

I think that such feelings are common to all of us when we are looking to the future, to events which will in some way change, alter our lives, to people with whom we will come in contact and who will influence us for good or for bad. I think such feelings are common to all of us as we anticipate being with a person known in one way in the past, to be known in quite a different way in the future.

That uncertain future. If only we could know for sure.

Wouldn't you agree that most people have a desire to know the future, to know what lies in store for them in the days and weeks and years ahead? But would you not also agree that some people, perhaps many people, hesitate, have ambivalent feelings about knowing the future? Maybe it's good; then again, maybe it's not good. I cannot speak for you but I think that is how I feel about knowing, looking into the future.

If I should happen to read the column in the daily newspaper entitled "Your stars today" (almost every newspaper in the land features such a column with a similar title), I read with a healthy skepticism. However—in the back of my mind I can detect the faint, unarticulated thought: maybe what the column has to say under my sign is true, has some sort of validity, will come to pass.

And is it not also true that we look somewhat warily at those who claim to predict the future? We may be openly and thoroughly skeptical about such claims. None the less many of us will listen to or read these predictions with the thought—faint suggestion though it may be—maybe these things will happen. Consider how many followers Jeane Dixon has, for example. Also consider the rather startling number of predictions she has made which have really come to be. Of course, as she herself readily admits, she has made predictions which have not materialized. Sometimes the very opposite of what she has predicted occurs.

In any case, she has a wide and variegated following because people do want to know the future, do seek to ascertain future events. Now I have no desire to brush aside the predictions of Jeane Dixon lightly or with a shrug of the shoulders. Her track record is far too good to be treated in so cavalier a fashion. Indeed, the reading of one of her visions was one of a number of factors in prompting the study which is the basis of this book you are now reading. In that vision Mrs. Dixon saw the coming of a great world leader who would bring peace and security, who would also be a worldwide religious leader. Without question, this was a vision of the Anti-Christ, the Abomination of Desolation; also that vision may well have been diabolically inspired. For all that, it has a definite validity. It has, also, a definite value if it will prompt us (as it has in the present case) to turn to God and His prophets to seek a more trustworthy presentation of future events.

Somehow or other, for the most part, our religious training has not included the reading of the great prophets of Israel. Indeed, many of us are more prone to read our future in a teacup. Now, again, I do not care to dismiss lightly the reading of the leaves. No. I had an aunt—my godmother—who could read the tea leaves, at times, with disturbing accuracy. My aunt was a great favorite with a small group of women who gathered together weekly, ostensibly to play bridge. I think the real reason they met was to talk and to have my aunt read their fortunes in the tea leaves.

This was, without question, an entertainment. This was, I am sure, a harmless enough pastime. But it illustrates the point I am trying to make. Here we have a group of good Catholic, Church-going ladies striving to probe into the future, albeit in jest. I wonder, on occasion, how much this was in jest and how much it was in earnest. I know that Aunt B___ always told good fortunes; if she saw something bad in the leaves, she would never say so.

So—there does exist in the minds of many people the idea that, in one way or another, the future can be foretold. Real trouble arises when a person strives, in a really serious manner, to divine the future and seeks to do so by using the powers of evil. Only God can know what the future is for us and only He can reveal that future should He choose to do so.

God has, in fact, revealed much of the future to us in His book, the Bible. There exists, however, one serious difficulty. Few of us bother with the Bible. Of the few who do read the Bible fewer still struggle with its prophetic books. I suppose it is really true. Reading tea leaves does tend to be simpler and more fun. Be that as it may, if we are really interested in knowing the future we had better turn to the one source who can provide it—God.

Peering into the future can be quite dangerous. You can fall prey to the powers of evil, to Satan, if you seek to know the future in the wrong manner and in the wrong places. This is no idle statement.

Consider: the ritual murders of children which have occurred during celebrations of the Black Mass; the suicides which have occurred because of Devil worship; the deaths (murders) which have occurred—through psychic suggestion, of course—by the invocation of the Devil (as in voodoo); hallucinations, mental aberrations, mental collapse, the obscene violation of sacred objects.

Consider: the title of a famous modern novel which does, indeed, deal with the development of false religion amongst a group of boys stranded on an island: Beelzebub—that is, The Lord of the Flies. Fascinating! Or would you care to learn of the worship of Satan so prevalent here in northeastern New Jersey? I can even give you a place: the Watchung Reservation at a desolate wooded area called, locally, Elephant's Graveyard. Devotees gather to worship the Devil. Two local girls were murdered only last year in the worship of Satan. Oh, yes. Satan is very much with us.

This is but a brief and mild listing of some events which have occurred because some human beings have sought the power not only to know the future but to influence and control the future, to bend the future to their own will.

All this has a long history. The history of Satanism, of Devil-worship, would seem to be co-extensive with the history of the human race. Yet it seems to me that such activities are very prevalent especially in today's world; they are growing in popularity and are practiced quite openly. Leaders of such cults can be seen on TV talk shows, worldwide conventions are held, books and magazines and articles dealing with the subject are readily available. Not a few of our colleges and universities offer courses in the subject. Of course, courses being offered in para-psychology can be quite legitimate and of great value. Yet even here such great caution is most advisable.

Seen now so briefly, you can well understand why I say there does exist a widespread interest in divining the future and, for some, an intense desire to control the future.

Let us turn now, just for a moment, to something that is, perhaps, a trifle more commonplace, some rather ordinary facts of life. I would think it safe to say that most of us participate in some sort of insurance or social security or pension plan, frequently from the moment of birth (sometimes even before birth) to the moment of death (and sometimes even after death).

We all live with statistics. Insurance statistics, educational statistics, employment statistics, health statistics, death statistics. The list could almost be indefinite. What are we doing? Why are so many of us so interested in these vast statistical systems—made possible with our complex computer technology?

We are trying to foretell the future, of course. In my mind there is no question about this. Given certain data, a set of statistics, we peer into the future, our future. Then by means of insurance, savings, social security—whatever—we try to provide for, defend, protect, in some way shape our future.

For much of our life we are constantly betting on the future and every one of us wants to bet on a sure thing. No, there is little question in my mind that the future does hold an intense interest for us and all of us, one way or another, do try to divine the future.

Of course, in using actuarial statistics, in using computer projections, in using data gathered in scientific samplings and under controlled conditions, we are, at least, using our God-given mental facilities to try to assess the future material aspects of our lives. This is to act in a prudent manner. It is a valid concern and activity.

It is when we turn to the future spiritual aspects of our lives that we seem to behave rather foolishly. We frequently look for valid and reasonable information in invalid and unreasonable places, persons, or things.

If we seek guidance for our material future, we surely should seek guidance for our spiritual future. I would suggest that we do have an institution, the Church, which can and does help us in these matters, frequently enough by affirming and exercising her role as guardian of the deposit of faith.

By way of example, let's talk about Fatima. Most of us, of course, have heard of Lourdes in France and of Our Blessed Lady's appearing to Saint Bernadette. The Miracle of Fatima is not as well known. I realize that many of you have heard of Fatima. However, a great number of people have not. In 1917 at Fatima in Portugal Our Blessed Lady appeared to three peasant children and revealed certain future events to them. Without getting lost in the story of Fatima, which is not my purpose here, it suffices to say that the Church has given its approval to devotion to Our Lady of Fatima. (As is always the case, in such matters, the message of Fatima is a private revelation. It may be accepted or rejected according to the dictates of one's own conscience.) Following World War I and up to the year 1960, devotion to Our Lady of Fatima grew, spreading throughout the world. As is so frequently the case, it was the extraordinary events which occurred at Fatima which attracted many, many people. Many amongst the devotees of Fatima had the impression that one of the so-called "secret" revelations of Fatima was to be made known by Church officials in the year 1960. When this did not occur they were disillusioned. The popularity of Fatima waned.

People, it seems, were much more interested in the extraordinary "secret" which was not made known than in the essential message of Fatima which was proclaimed openly, clearly, simply. "Repent; do penance; the kingdom of God is at hand." This is and will ever remain the real message of Our Lady, no matter where she appears, no matter what the extraordinary manifestations of her appearance. But it is precisely this message that we choose to ignore. It does not quite represent the future we had or have in mind. None the less, the future is being made manifest through the auspices of Our Lady. The future and how to prepare for it are there for us to see. As to whether or not we accept the guidance being offered depends on us and our own free will.

Another apparition of Our Lady, not at all well known at the present time, occurred at La Salette in France in 1846. A rather small group of quite determined devotees strives to promulgate the message of La Salette in their own fashion. It is certainly true that you find many similarities in the messages of La Salette and Fatima. But at La Salette future events are set forth in far greater detail. Now I do not wish to undermine the prophetic message which you may or may not be able to glean from the varied and rather garbled transmissions of that message. I would like to point out, however, that while details about future events are certainly fascinating, the essential message of La Salette, almost totally over- looked, is: "Repent; do penance; the kingdom of God is at hand." But as is so often the case, it is the extraordinary events which claim our attention; the call to penance is readily ignored.

Yet other hazards exist regarding the La Salette story. Early ver- sions restrict the events and the message to the place and time of their occurrence. Later versions, later publications see the message as applying to the people of every age and especially to people living in the latter days of this present age.

For some people the message would seem to deal with problems in France in the last century. This is a natural stance to take since apparently many of the dire famines and plagues of the last century were foretold at La Salette. Yet much of what Our Lady apparently said would seem to apply to the latter days and to those living in those days—in a word, seemingly to us.

Might it not be a good idea to check out the uncertainties of private revelation against the certainties of the public revelation as contained in the Holy Scriptures?

Private revelations are, of course, not a new phenomenon in the Church. One of the teaching offices of the early Church was the prophetic office. St. Paul speaks of this. St. Paul himself exercised that office, as the inspired texts of his epistles are frequently prophetic in nature. Naturally when we speak of St. Paul's prophecies, or St. John's, or any of the Old or New Testament prophets—Our Lord most especially, we must understand that we are dealing with public revelation. We have here the inspired au- thority of Scripture and the inspired Tradition of the Church.

Private revelation is another matter. The teaching Church very prudently exercises extreme caution in accepting or rejecting all private revelation.

Subject, then, to the Church's approval, it would seem that a number of people are being granted private revelations in today's world concerning the LATTER DAYS, the anti-Christ (the Abomination of Desolation), the RAPTURE, the persecution of the Church, the Second Coming of Our Lord, ARMAGEDDON, and Our Lord's thousand-year reign known as the Millennium.

Some of these private revelations are quite clearly inspired by the Devil. This is precisely why such caution must be exercised about private revelation. Without question certain revelations which have occurred in Spain, in Mexico, and in the United States have been the Devil's work. However, other revelations are occurring in various places around the world which seem to be God's work.

Again, some private revelations occurring in Spain, perhaps in Mexico, in France, perhaps in the United States (Brooklyn, New York) may be genuine. Perhaps they can serve as guides in charting certain future events (subject always to the authority of the Church).

Private revelations at the village of Garabandal in Spain will serve to illustrate the point. In the years 1961 through 1965 four children of the village of Garabandal apparently were the recipients of messages from Our Lady. Despite the rather strange behavior of the children—behavior which causes a very legitimate question mark as to the validity of the events at Garabandal—the message is decidedly valid in itself. The central and essential message of Garabandal is: "We must do much penance and make many sacrifices. We must often visit the Blessed Sacrament. But, above all, we must be very good for, if we are not, we will be punished. The cup is already filling and if we do not amend our lives there will come a great chastisement."

The devotees of Garabandal do seem to place some stress upon the importance of this message, the necessity to act upon this message. However, it is also true that the message seems to get lost in the ever proliferating literature about Garabandal. You could easily receive the impression that a greater stress, a greater interest, surrounds the promise of a miracle to come and the warning which will occur prior to that miracle. The punishments to be meted out should the Garabandal message be ignored are also high-lighted.

Admittedly all the talk of warnings and miracles and punishments is considerably more fascinating than the talk of penance and sacrifice. It is, once again, a very human thing for the followers of

Garabandal to stress the promised "great miracle." It seems a most natural reaction to gloss over the "warning" prior to the "miracle." Yet if Garabandal is genuine then it is very possible that the so-called "warning" is the RAPTURE of which St. Paul speaks in second Corinthians, Chapter Five. If this is the case (and it probably is) then the "warning" of Garabandal will be a worldwide phenomenon of the greatest possible importance. So, too, the "miracle." Apparently Russia will be converted as a result of it. But the "warning" is equally important.

Thus viewed in the light of public revelation as contained in the Holy Scriptures, private revelation (at Garabandal and elsewhere) begins to assume some order and acquires a certain clarity not usually intrinsic to itself.

It is rather unfortunate, so it seems to me, that no modern Catholic commentaries are available for Church members to consult about these things. A few old, really dated, volumes can be obtained. They are so poor or so out of date that, in good conscience, I cannot recommend them. And, of course, so-called "liberal" Catholics and Protestants rather look down their noses at this entire subject. Which leaves fundamentalist Protestants. Sure enough. There are quite a number of books about the latter days by fundamentalist Protestants, many of them quite good indeed. While theologians and scripture scholars of the Catholic Church have paid little attention to the Book of Revelation, the last book of the New Testament and such books of the Old Testament as Ezekiel, Daniel, some of the minor prophets—saying merely that these books are largely symbolic in nature, Protestant theologians and scripture scholars have produced an extensive library in Biblical prophecy and revelation.

Some of these books are popular; some are scholarly. For example, *The Late Great Planet Earth* and *There's a New World Coming* by Hal Lindsey seem to be based on reasonably solid scholarship. They are written in light journalistic style. While these books are easy to read they could not serve as source material for a scholarly dissertation on the latter days. Somewhat similar treatment will be found in such books as *The Last and Future World* by Boice and *The King Is Coming* by Willington.

Three books by Arthur E. Bloomfield are serious studies, scholarly works without question. Bloomfield really does an extensive, in-depth study of Bible prophecy. I wish that I could recommend them to you. I cannot. The author is so vehemently biased against the Catholic Church that his books suffer the embarrassment of personal distortion. A pity, really, because he has some worthwhile things to say.

Among the many other studies that could be mentioned I would like to suggest that J. Dwight Pentecost's book *Things to Come* is worthy of serious consideration. While it is true that we disagree with several of his arguments and conclusions, his book is, nevertheless, an astonishing compilation of the serious (Protestant) research in this area of Bible prophecy and the latter days.

So far as I know we Catholics do not have anything like Pentecost's book, offering guidance and guidelines about the end-time, the latter days of this present Church age. However, we do have the liturgy of the Mass which can be and is a reasonably effective way of teaching us the truths of the gospel. As you are probably well aware, that part of the Mass which includes the first and second readings and the gospel reading is called, now, the Liturgy of the Word. Hopefully these readings are helping us to know and understand the truths proclaimed in the Old and New Testaments.

Even prior to the many changes which have been going on in the Church since the Second Vatican Council, some instruction was offered about the latter days. Those of us who are on the older side of—say about 30—can recall, if we were regular in our Mass attendance, the gospels for the last Sunday of the year and for the first Sunday of Advent. "When you see the abomination of desolation, which was spoken of by Daniel the prophet, standing in the holy place . . . ," these are lines which remain vividly in the memory. Phrases such as "But woe to those who are with child, or have infants at the breast in those days! But pray that your flight may not be in the winter or on the Sabbath" have a certain startling, even frightening effect.

That gospel passage (St. Matthew, Chapter 24, Verses 15–35) read on the last Sunday of the Church year served as a very salutary reminder that we did not have here a lasting city. In light of that gospel we were given to understand that this world would come to an end. Just when that end would come was not clear. However it was pointed out that, since we did not know the exact day or hour of the end, it might be well to be always prepared for such an eventuality.

Too, while the events described in St. Matthew's Gospel were pushed into the uncertain future, the gospel served very well to remind us of our own personal end—our own death and the moment of our own particular judgment. These were certain facts. Death could claim us at any moment in the more or less immediate future. Therefore, heed the message: repent; do penance; the kingdom of God is at hand.

The gospel reading for the first Sunday of the year was from St. Luke, Chapter 21, Verses 25–33. This gospel sounded a more helpful note but the theme of repentance, penance, sorrow for sin was very much a part of the message. In those days the advent season was a penitential season, a time to cleanse oneself of sin, thus preparing one's soul for the coming birth of Our Lord on Christmas day. The gospel itself did point to future events concerning the latter days. However the stress was: preparation for the Christmas season. Not that this was bad. Certainly it is always necessary to do penance and repent of one's sins. God can call us home at any moment. It is best to be prepared.

Yet consider the sentence: "But when these things begin to come to pass, look up and lift up your heads, because your redemption is at hand." This refers to our attitude when we see the signs of the approach of the latter days. Given the context of the Advent season that prophetic element was not stressed. The emphasis was placed on the historical event of Our Lord's birth. This was the redemption of which the gospel spoke, not some other future occurrence.

Such spiritual symbolism surely has its place in interpreting the Sacred Scriptures. However I must hasten to add that the literal sense of the Scriptures should not, on that account, be voided or vitiated.

Certainly we should lift up our heads and rejoice when we are about to celebrate the anniversary of the historical birth of Our Lord. Certainly we should look up and exult when we are about to celebrate the spiritual birth of Our Lord within our souls. But we should not neglect the literal meaning of the text: when we notice those certain signs which portend that the latter days are at hand we are to stand erect, we are to look up and we are to lift up our heads that we may greet Our Lord with great joy and exultation as He returns upon the clouds with great power and majesty.

But the gospel commentaries of those days did not particularly stress or even mention the prophetic and literal meaning of the gospel. It is the same today. Modern commentaries, homiletic materials, tend to shy away from a literal interpretation of the prophetic texts of the Old and New Testaments which are now used as a part of the Mass in the Liturgy of the Word.

Since the revised Liturgy contains readings of a prophetic nature which deal with the latter days, it seems a rather serious oversight that the People of God are not being properly instructed as to the basic root meaning of the Word of God.

It seems to me that it is of no small import that, in the revised liturgy, even the Ordinary of the Mass (that part of the Mass which remains more or less the same) and the Prefaces of the Mass contain a number of references to the Second Coming of Our Lord.

Now it may be said that what the liturgical specialists had in mind when restructuring the Mass texts was a greater harmony with and a more accurate reflection of the primitive and early Church, thus reflecting better the mind and will of Our Lord. So the liturgists may have reasoned, and rightly so.

The thought occurs to me, however, that the Holy Spirit may have had other ideas vis-à-vis the restructuring of the Mass in these present times. Perhaps, under the guidance of the Holy Spirit, the time has arrived to take a closer and much more serious look at the Bible prophecies concerning the latter days.

In any case, a number of the new Prefaces refer clearly and certainly to the Second Coming for which we are (here and now!) joyfully awaiting. The standard memorial acclamations refer to and now bring to mind our belief that "Christ will come again." Eucharistic prayer three makes the bold statement: "And ready to greet Him when He comes again." Eucharistic prayer four also has similar phrases. After the recitation of the Our Father the priest says: "Deliver us, Lord, from every evil, and grant us peace in our day. In your mercy keep us free from sin and protect us from all anxiety AS WE WAIT IN JOYFUL HOPE FOR THE COMING OF OUR SAVIOUR, JESUS CHRIST."

I could continue with many other quotations and allusions. However the message is clear enough: the Second Coming of Our Lord is very much a part of the revised liturgy.

While the liturgy in and of itself is quite clear, it is the many and ever proliferating commentaries on the Mass texts which cause concern and not a little confusion. A creative worship service for the thirty-second Sunday of the year, for example, suggests a homily on 1st Thessalonians, Chapter 4, Verses 13–18. The homily, good in itself, asks the believing Christian to look at death and specifically his or her own death. This is, as I say, good. However, the homily says absolutely nothing about the real, the literal meaning of St. Paul's words which are prophetic words dealing with the Second Coming of Our Lord. Astonishing!

Again, just by way of example, let's look at the second reading for the thirty-third Sunday of the year. First Thessalonians, Chapter 5, Verses 1–6, are prophetic words of St. Paul treating of the latter days and the manner of the Second Coming of Our Lord. In the suggested homily there is nary a word about this.

The Church's revised liturgy is trying to teach us about the latter days and Our Lord's Second Coming. The commentaries on the Mass texts negate, so it seems to me, everything the revised liturgy is trying to do.

In one series of commentaries which purports to serve as a guide for the People of God it is fascinating to see certain selections from the prophet Ezekiel relegated to the past when, in fact, the selections refer very clearly to the end-times and have not yet occurred. In the same series the book of Daniel is treated as a fictional story concocted to inspire Jews of the 2nd Century, B.C. Yet Our Lord Himself refers to the prophecies of Daniel, in St. Matthew, Chapter 24, Verses 15–35, as though they were real prophecies and He expected them to come true at some future time.

I think I shall opt for Our Lord's version of Daniel. And I think I shall opt for the emphasis placed upon the prophetic texts of the Bible in the early Church. It is one thing to use the same texts in the Mass as did the early and primitive Church; it is quite another thing to use these texts in the same manner, with the same meaning. Pius Parsch, in his famed commentary so popular back in the 1950's, points out that early Christians of the first, second, and third centuries were very conscious of Our Lord's Second Coming, of the Parousia. Later, by the time of the middle ages, the emphasis on the Parousia, the Second Coming, had been changed. The emphasis, at that point, was on the present order of grace, on the Church as the Kingdom, on the personal death of believers as the moment to be awaited in fear and trembling.

Parsch makes this fascinating, and very true, observation: "The Second Coming is wrapped in such obscurity that seldom did we dare to speak of it."

Speaking of Advent, Parsch says: "Now we more readily see the truth: Advent is really a continuation of the Church's autumn season, her preparation for the Savior's return. In this light Christmas and Epiphany are one great feast oriented to the Parousia."

It is important to note that, underlying the historical version of the liturgy acquired in medieval times, the essential thrust of the liturgy is the Parousia. It is also important to note that the Second Coming was viewed as incomprehensible and beyond the scope of our human intellects. This certainly is in accord with the words in the book of Daniel (Dan. 12:9), "Go, Daniel, . . . because the words are to be kept secret and sealed until the end-time."

It is only now—in these very days in which we are living—that we are able to understand much of what Daniel wrote about. Too, many of us are aware of a greater stress being given St. John's Book of Revelation. We are—now—able to understand many of the things he wrote about, recording Our Lord's own words in fact, in the Book of the Apocalypse. The prophetic books of the Old and New Testaments concerning the latter days are unfolding, are being unsealed, as historical events foretold thousands of years ago are being fulfilled NOW—in these our times.

I suppose I should mention, at least in passing, that the Second Vatican Council, in its treatment on the constitution of the Church, deals specifically with the eschatological nature of the Pilgrim Church. The Council speaks of the Church (that is, all of us) as awaiting the promised restoration begun already in Christ. The final age of the world has already come upon us and the Church Herself dwells among those groaning and travailing in pain until now, awaiting the glory to come, when the Lord comes in His majesty, and all the angels with Him.

I must note, with some interest, that the revised Liturgy of the Hours (the Divine Office) makes use of a number of passages from the Council. One example: "While helping the world and receiving many benefits from it, the Church has a single intention: that God's kingdom may come, and that the salvation of the whole human race may come to pass . . . The Lord Himself speaks: 'Behold, I come quickly! And my reward is with me, to render to each one according to his works. I am the Alpha and the Omega, the first and the last, the beginning and the end' (Rev. 22:12–13)."

The Church's Liturgy of the Hours, at least, surely re-enforces one aspect of the teaching of the Second Vatican Council which is almost totally ignored: the Second Coming of Our Lord and the establishment of His kingdom. So the Council states: "On this earth (Our Lord's) kingdom is already present in mystery. When the Lord returns it will be brought into full flower."

Part II

The More Certain
Prophetic Light

The Advent liturgy includes readings from the prophet Isaiah, from the second Book of Samuel, from the prophet Jeremiah, the prophet Baruch, Zephaniah, the prophet Micah. New Testament readings include readings from St. Paul, St. James, St. Peter. The gospel readings, as you might well expect, are selected from all four gospels. These readings are arranged in a three-year cycle, but, again, I am telling you something you already know.

In the first reading of the first Sunday of Advent, year A, the selection is from Isaiah (Is. 2:1–5). It is used, in the liturgy, in a symbolic and spiritual sense. Literally the text is, without question, eschatological in nature and is a prophecy concerning the end-time. In the second reading for that Sunday St. Paul tells us: "The night is far spent; the day draws near" (Rom. 13:11–14). St. Paul is referring to the Second Coming. The gospel you already know; it is Our Lord's prophecy of the latter days.

On the second Sunday of Advent the reading is, again, from Isaiah (Is. 11:1–10). In this selection we see a prophetic text PARTIALLY fulfilled in Our Lord, His historical presence upon earth. Complete fulfillment will occur at the end-times. (Even a casual reading is enough to know immediately that much of the prophetic text has yet to be fulfilled.)

In the second reading for the third Sunday of Advent St. James tells us: "Be patient, my brothers, until the coming of the Lord" (Jas. 5:7–10). And so it goes. I could go on and on. Of thirty-six possible readings well over half are quite clearly eschatological in nature and deal directly or indirectly with the Second Coming of Our Lord. St. Paul tells us, by way of another example, in the selection for the second reading of the first Sunday of Advent, year C, of the Second Coming. He prays: "May the Lord increase you and make you overflow with love for one another and for all, even as our love for you does. May He strengthen your hearts, making them blameless and holy before our God and Father *at the coming of Our Lord Jesus with His holy ones*" (1 Thess. 3:12–14).

Of course, when we turn to the liturgy of the Christmas—Epiphany season, many of the historical events of Our Lord's earthly life are presented and commemorated. This is as it should be. However—once again, an underlying, ever present eschatological theme can be noted. On the very day of Christmas itself, the varied first and second readings treat of the latter days and refer directly to Our Lord's Second Coming. The readings from the prophet Isaiah, while used symbolically to refer to Our Lord's historical birth, really refer to the time of the latter days.

St. Paul in his letter to Titus, the second reading of the Christmas Midnight Mass, says: "The grace of God has appeared, offering salvation to all men. It trains us to reject godless ways and worldly desires, and live temperately, justly, and devoutly in this age *as we await our blessed hope, the appearing of the glory of the great God and of Our Savior Christ Jesus.* It was he who sacrificed himself for us, to redeem us from all unrighteousness and to cleanse for himself a people of his own, eager to do what is right" (Tit. 2:11–14).

The gospels of the season, of course, show us the historical fulfillment of prophecies about Our Lord. They thus sustain us in our belief that the prophecies made by Isaiah and the other Biblical prophets concerning the latter days will also be fulfilled to the letter.

The first readings of Epiphany and of the Baptism of Our Lord are clearly eschatological in nature and need no further comment from me.

And I note, in passing, that the varied texts used in the weekday Masses of Advent, too numerous to comment upon, are—again, I must use the phrase—eschatological in nature. They serve to confirm the opinion that the Advent liturgy very definitely focuses attention upon the Second Coming of Our Lord.

Many of the Bible texts used in the Advent season are from Isaiah, that prophet of God who lived just about 2700 years ago, give or take a few years. He was born about 765 B.C. When he was about twenty-five years old, therefore, and while he was in the Temple of Jerusalem God gave Isaiah the command to go forth and prophesy to the Israelites. He was to proclaim to them the Lord's message and their fate should they neglect the message. Beyond these scant facts, it is known that Isaiah was the son of Amoz, that he married, had two sons, that he lived in Jerusalem where he exercised the prophetic office for a period of about forty years. Apparently he was, in some way, attached to or connected with the royal household for he had easy access to the kings of Israel and was an advisor to them, especially in their moments of crisis.

It is surely interesting to know that Isaiah was a poetical genius and wrote in splendid style. What is of far greater moment, for us, is his prophetic message. To Isaiah we ascribe the famous prophecy of Our Lord's virginal birth (Isaiah 7:14). To him we also ascribe many messianic prophecies which found fulfillment in Our Lord, the famed "Suffering Servant" passages for example.

Isaiah's book falls into two principal divisions:

(1) Chapters 1 to 39 look toward the Assyrian captivity.

(2) Chapters 40 to 66 look toward deliverance and future blessings.

It is certainly true that much of what Isaiah wrote pertains to the rather immediate historical events of his own times. Many passages, of course, pertain to the historical events of Our Lord's life while He was yet on this earth. However, many, many passages speak, quite clearly, of the latter days, the end-times. One example: Isaiah, Chapter 11. While part of that chapter can be applied to Our Lord and sees the messianic age as beginning with Our Lord's historical life, it is very obvious that much of that prophetic chapter has not been fulfilled. You are, then, forced to decide: either Isaiah is a prophet (or, at least, the book ascribed to Isaiah is a prophetic book) or Isaiah is not a prophet (or the book ascribed to Isaiah is not a prophetic book). If it is not a prophetic book—THEN—a whole series of disconcerting things happen to Biblical inspiration, Biblical inerrancy, God's truth, God's Church, the teaching-prophesying-believing liturgy, the guidance of the Holy Spirit, and et cetera and et cetera and et cetera. Fascinating! No, it won't do. If this is not prophecy the entire structure built upon Scripture and Tradition starts to crumble and you would be entirely justified in turning your back on the whole sorry mess. But this is nonsense and offends my common sense.

It *is* prophecy, the foundations *are* sound and the entire structure *does* stand. Applied common sense says: some of the prophecies have been fulfilled. Therefore the prophecies not yet fulfilled *will be* fulfilled and when the prophet says they will be fulfilled—namely, *in that day*. We can only add—given the re-establishment of the nation of Israel—that it looks as if *in that day* is fast becoming *in these our days*.

Jeremiah, too, was a prophet of the Lord and selections from his book of prophecy are used in the Advent liturgy. And, once again, much of what Jeremiah wrote applies to his own time. Yet much of what he prophesied looks beyond his own time, and even the historical time of Our Lord's physical presence upon this planet earth, to the latter days, the end-times, the millennial kingdom.

The prophet's life is not an easy one and Jeremiah's lot was to suffer and die a martyr's death. (Apparently he was stoned to death. There is a legend that Isaiah, too, died a martyr's death by being sawn in two. Neither of the two sounds like a particularly pleasant way to die.)

Jeremiah lived about a century after Isaiah. He was born about 646 B.C. He was from a priestly family which lived near Jerusalem. He received the prophet's office, while yet a youth, in 626 B.C.

During Jeremiah's lifetime a number of catastrophic events befell his nation and the city of Jerusalem itself. Nebuchadnezzar besieged the city and deported many of its inhabitants. The Temple was destroyed in another later siege. Throughout all this Jeremiah prophesied, preached, threatened disaster—in vain. Even his book, which Jeremiah had dictated to his secretary, Baruch, was burned by King Jehaiakim. The entire book had to be rewritten, as it was by that faithful secretary, and prophet in his own right, Baruch.

The book of Jeremiah, therefore, contains present and future prophecies about Judah, Jerusalem, and, also, the nations. Consider Jeremiah, Chapter 23, Verses 5–8: "Behold, the days are coming, says the Lord, when I will raise up for David a righteous branch and he shall reign as king and deal wisely, and shall execute justice and righteousness in the land. In his days Judah will be saved, and Israel will dwell securely. And this is the name by which he will be called: 'The Lord is our righteousness.'

"Therefore, behold, the days are coming, says the Lord, when men shall no longer say, 'as the Lord lives who brought up the people of Israel out of the land of Egypt,' but 'as the Lord lives who brought up and led the descendants of the house of Israel out of the north country and out of all the countries where he had driven them.' Then they shall dwell in their own land."

Here again, either Jeremiah is a prophet or he is not. If he is not he is not worth bothering about. And his message, the essential prophetic message: "Repent, do penance," is not worth bothering about either. But he did utter prophecy which has been fulfilled. Therefore his prophecies which have not yet been fulfilled, as in the example I just gave you, will be fulfilled. Proof of the prophecy is the fulfillment of it.

The third of the major prophets of the Old Testament, Ezekiel, had some rather strange things to say and to do in his role as prophet. Of course, Isaiah had to walk around naked for several years, thus graphically depicting the future and utter desolation of Jerusalem and its haughty inhabitants. I have often wondered if he had to wander about stark naked or whether he was allowed to wear a loin cloth of some sort, at least. Which, of course, is neither here nor there, and has nothing to do with Ezekiel, in any case.

Ezekiel was one of the exiled Israelites who dwelt in Babylon and who received the prophetic office by the river Chebar. He was struck dumb at that time and had to mime his various prophecies, as God directed him. He had to lie on his left side for one hundred and ninety days and then on his right side for forty days, thus to bear the sins of the house of Israel and the sins of the house of Judah. He had to dig a hole in a wall and go out through it, having packed an exile's bundle, thus depicting the departure of the exiles. With these signs plus his reproaches, Ezekiel preached God's message to the house of Israel and also to all the citizens of Jerusalem.

But there is more to Ezekiel than prophecies already fulfilled.

Certain of his visions (labeled now by modern scholars as apocalyptic—by which term they seem to imply that his visions have no prophetic value) deal with the latter days and the millennial kingdom. For example, the 37th chapter of Ezekiel. Will those famous dry bones live? Is Ezekiel a prophet or not? Those dry bones will live and, moreover, Judah and Israel will be one, they will be gathered from everywhere and they will be brought home to their own soil and they will be one nation.

That's a pretty good résumé of the current events of the past twenty-five years in the near east—considering it was written about twenty-five hundred years ago.

I would like, next, to have you consider the Book of Daniel, the fourth and last of the major Old Testament prophets. But first let me give you a brief rundown on the minor prophets of the Old Testament, if only because the minor prophets are now included in the various readings of the revised liturgy of the Mass. These minor prophets were but little heard of, if at all, in those ancient, long-ago days of pre-Vatican II. Who among us who is over 30 or 35 ever heard of Habakkuk or Obadiah? Who is Haggai? These minor prophets are now included in the revised liturgy. (I must hasten to tell you that these men are labeled minor simply because they wrote little, short books.)

Amos, a shepherd of Tekoa, came out of the hill country to denounce social injustice, insincere ceremonial rites, among other things, and to foretell dire punishment for infidelity. It is in the book of Amos that the phrase "the Day of Yahweh" first occurs in the Bible. And it is Amos who, in his dreadful omens, speaks of Israel's downfall, but who also foretells of the return of the Jewish people to their land.

Hosea, a contemporary of Amos, was a native of the northern kingdom. He married Gomar who became a prostitute, thus symbolizing the unfaithfulness of the Israelite nation toward the Lord God. Yet Hosea took Gomar back. So, too, will God take Israel back. The Jewish nation will be cast forth from the land, but it will be restored *in the latter days*. St. Paul himself said that such a restoration would occur as he makes quite clear in Romans 11:26.

Micah, prophesying about 721 B.C., was a contemporary of both Hosea and Isaiah. However, he was quite independent of either. He, like Amos, was a peasant and was quite suspicious and contemptuous of city life. Micah, one with the other prophets, foretold disaster because of the corruption of the people. But, as always, his message incorporates hope for the future.

Obadiah foresees the eventual triumph of Israel "in the day of

Yahweh," but Zephaniah utters some really dreadful prophecies about the nations "in the day of Yahweh."

The books of Nahum and Jonah predict the punishment of Assyria and the eventual destruction of Nineveh. And you well know, of course, that Our Lord uses the adventures related in the book of Jonah as a symbol of his own death and resurrection.

The prophets Haggai, Zechariah, and Malachi may be grouped together in that Haggai and Zechariah urge the restoration of the temple in post-exilic Jerusalem. More than this, these prophets look toward a future Messiah and the hope of a messianic age.

The prophecies of Malachi are of a somewhat different nature. Castigating the failures of priests and people in their religious duties, he, nevertheless, foresees the day of the Messiah and the restoration of the moral order. The perfect sacrifice will be offered by the gentile nations "from the rising of the sun even to its setting" for the Lord's name is great among the nations.

It is Malachi who says that before the "day of Yahweh" occurs the Lord will send Elijah the prophet. Our Blessed Lord applied this prophecy to St. John the Baptist since St. John came in the Spirit of Elijah. There will, however, be a literal fulfillment of the prophecy since Elijah is to return prior to that great and terrible day. (A goodly number of Church Fathers so believed: Cyril, Chrysostom, Augustine, Jerome—and also Tertullian, Theodoret.) And this prophecy will come to pass since Malachi foresaw not only the events of Our Lord's first coming upon the earth, but also the events of His Second Coming.

Little is known of the prophet Joel. He exercised the prophetic office probably around 400 B.C. The liturgy, very naturally, uses his prophetic message especially during the lenten season since it is Joel who preaches repentance and the physical acts of atonement, fasting and the donning of sack-cloth.

"Come, pass the night in sack-cloth, you ministers of my God . . . Order a fast, proclaim a solemn assembly . . ."

It is Joel, too, who proclaims: "The Day of Yahweh is near in the Valley of Decision!"

And in Acts 2:17, St. Peter uses the prophecy of Joel almost verbatim:

After this I will pour out my spirit on ALL mankind. Your sons and daughters shall prophesy, your old men shall dream dreams, and your young men shall see visions.

Even on the slaves, men and women, will I pour out my spirit in those days. I will display portents in heaven and on earth, blood and fire and columns of smoke.

The sun will be turned into darkness, and the moon into blood, before the day of Yahweh dawns, that great and terrible day. All who call on the name of Yahweh will be saved . . . for on Mount Zion will be some who have escaped, as Yahweh has said, and in Jerusalem some survivors whom Yahweh will call (Joel 3:1–5). JB

This passage, used on the Vigil of Pentecost, was, indeed, partially fulfilled on that first Pentecost nearly two thousand years ago. It has not yet been totally fulfilled and this gives us a clue or two about the end-times. With the breaking of the 6th seal (as recorded in St. John's Apocalypse) there will occur, as Joel says, a day of darkness. At this time the Russian invasion of Israel will occur. The Russian army will meet with defeat. THEN there will be the outpouring of the Spirit on ALL people. Still later yet another day of darkness will occur, the fifth trumpet-bowl of St. John. Then occurs the third day of darkness of which Joel speaks. This heralds the war of wars—Armageddon.

The Book of Revelation (or, as we say, the Apocalypse) supplies us with some of the fine details of the events of the latter days, the day of the Lord. Too, while we may not have the detailed description we might like, we do have a very fine presentation of the sequence of events of the latter days.

The ten and a half years between the RAPTURE and ARMAGEDDON and the Second Coming will be devastating.

I don't know about you but I hope I am caught up to meet the Lord at the time of the Rapture. I hope I am prepared for that sudden and unknown moment. The time after the Rapture is going to be one bloody mess. No—the clue very definitely is: be ready for the Rapture.

And now, just a word or two about the prophet Daniel. The new liturgy has fairly extensive readings from the Apocalypse of St. John and also from the prophet Daniel. As the introductory remarks in the Lectionary (the book which contains the varied readings of the first part of the Mass) say: "The books of Daniel and Revelations are assigned to the end of the Liturgical year since they have appropriate eschatological (end-time) themes."

So they do, and a goodly number of selections from both books are read during the last weeks of the year. In the divine office, however, the new Liturgy of the Hours, the Book of Revelations is read starting right after the Octave of Easter, which is interesting. Not that the Doctrine of the Second Coming, and also the Divine Indwelling, is anything new in the spiritual life of the Church. By way of example, St. Therese of Lisieux was well aware of these doctrines and they were an important part of her spiritual development. As a child she would sit with her father on a Sunday evening and listen to one of her sisters read from Dom Gueranger's *Liturgical Year*. In volume one (page 136 in my edition), for example, Gueranger speaks of the fear we may experience at the time of the Second Coming, but then describes the great joy we will have when we meet, face to face, the One who dwells within us.

Naturally enough, selections from Daniel and Revelations are read on the last Sunday of the year, the Feast of Christ the King. In both books we have vivid accounts of Our Lord's Second Coming. He is seen as one who is the Son of Man coming on the clouds of Heaven; His kingdom shall be forever.

A lot of arguing goes on amongst scripture scholars as to the dating of the book of Daniel and of Revelations, as to the authors of the books, about their prophetic content as opposed to their "apocalyptic" style. All of which is fun and a way of passing the time, but the time is getting short. In a word, it would seem that we began to run out of time at some point during the past thirty years. I strongly suspect that we do not have the time to be playing games. At the time of judgment Our Lord is not going to ask: "What did this or that scripture scholar say ABOUT the Scriptures?" No! He is going to ask: "What did I say in MY book and what have YOU done about it? Have YOU followed my suggestions, obeyed my commands?"

It is time for all of us to get back to the basic Gospel Truth. And it is the New Revised Liturgy—with its extensive Bible readings— which is—finally—helping us to do just that.

II

Part I
Now Hear the Word
of the Lord

Before I start discussing the latter days, the end-time with you, I think I had better go over a few preliminary, introductory notions. I feel fairly sure that many of you will already know what I'm talking about. However, for the sake of a reader here or there who may not possess much in the way of biblical background, a few preliminary thoughts are, perhaps, in order.

First and foremost, *Inspiration*. The Bible is the word of God. It has God for its principal author, joining forces with human authors to achieve His desired purpose, the Bible. All discussion of inspiration, nowadays, must still take into account, must still meet the criteria, set down by Pope Leo XIII in a very famous Encyclical entitled "Providentissimus Deus." In that Encyclical (or letter, if you prefer) the Pope said:

God so moved the inspired writers by His supernatural operation that He incited them to write, and assisted them in their writing so that they correctly conceived, accurately wrote down and truthfully expressed all that He intended; and only thus can God be the author of the Bible.

Thus it is that God authors the books of the Bible, using human authors to achieve His purposes. We may say, in the language of scholastic theology, that God is the principal cause, the human being is the instrumental cause, both cooperating to produce the final effect—to wit, the Bible.

Since God is its principal author, the Bible tells us what God wants us to know. But, it tells us so in the language, the idiom, the

vocabulary, the style (or lack of style) of the human author. All is
God's word and God's word does come to us in a variety of voices.
Rough, primitive, cultured, sophisticated, learned, rude, witty,
dull—all these voices achieve God's desired purpose, the writing
down of His desires for us, for each one of us individually, for all of
us together. He reveals to us, in these written words, His concep-
tion of Salvation history. Not that the Bible is merely a history book.
It is not. Rather it is a book about love, God's great wonderful love
for us His people.

  It is clear that the Bible is God's word. It has God as its author.
The Bible, however, is not *a* book. It is a series of books, a library, if
you will. How did it happen that these books were gathered together to form that one volume library we label the Bible? Many
books, after all, proclaim that they are the written word of God.
How, then, did *this* selection as opposed to *that* selection become
part of our Bible? And, after all, as Bishop John J. Dougherty (our
"old" scripture prof) says: "The books of the Bible were composed
by many individuals or schools over a period that spans more than a
thousand years, when we consider the phase of oral tradition and
early written documents. It must also be noted that the Bible was
finished almost two thousand years ago. It comes down to this:
when you read the Bible you are reading an ancient library of books
written roughly between 1250 B.C. and A.D. 100" (p. 20).[1]

  As far as we are concerned the question was settled by the Coun-
cil of Trent back in 1546 A.D.—on April 8th of that year. That Coun-
cil declared that it accepted as the books of the Canon of the Old
Testament: Genesis, Exodus, Leviticus, Numbers, Deuteronomy,
Joshua, Judges, Ruth, 1 Samuel, 2 Samuel, 1 Kings, 2 Kings, 1
Chronicles, 2 Chronicles, Ezra, Nehemiah, Tobit, Judith, Esther,
Job, Psalms, Proverbs, Ecclesiastes, Song of Songs, Wisdom,
Sirach, Isaiah, Jeremiah, Lamentations, Baruch, Ezekiel, Daniel,
Hosea, Joel, Amos, Obadiah, Jonah, Micah, Nahum, Habakkuk,
Zephaniah, Haggai, Zechariah, Malachi, 1 Maccabees, 2 Mac-
cabees.

  On that very same day the council defined the canon of the New
Testament: St. Matthew, St. Mark, St. Luke, St. John, Acts of the
Apostles, Romans, 1 Corinthians, 2 Corinthians, Galatians, Ephe-
sians, Philippians, Colossians, 1 Thessalonians, 2 Thessalonians, 1
Timothy, 2 Timothy, Titus, Philemon, Hebrews, St. James, 1 St.
Peter, 2 St. Peter, 1 St. John, 2 St. John, 3 St. John, St. Jude, Revela-
tion.

[1] Dougherty, *Searching the Scriptures,* Doubleday, N.Y., 1959.

Of course these books, by and large, had been accepted as composing the Bible for a fair number of centuries before the Council of Trent. But the Council of Trent did tend to make things rather definitive, to say nothing of definite.

In a word, the canon of the Bible is determined by the living, teaching Church whose tradition includes and presents to us God's revealed truth by means of the spoken and the written word.

The apostles made use of the books of the Old Testament, as did Our Blessed Lord. All they really did was simply to use the collection of sacred books used in their synagogues or in the Temple. That collection grew gradually over the years and, in time, was arranged according to a threefold division: the Law, the Prophets, and the Writings. One collection of these books became very famous, a collection called the Septuagint. It was this version of the Bible which was almost certainly the Bible of the Apostolic Church.

Of course, the Apostles and Evangelists wrote about the life of Our Lord. They wrote down His Teachings and these written accounts of Our Lord's life and Teachings were quickly accepted as being sacred also. By the year 150 A.D. the New Testament was accepted as Scripture, a sacred book, as were the books of the Old Testament.

Thus briefly, we have a book or rather a collection of books. And we know them, accept them as God's word because of our belief in, our devotion to God's Church.

I have stressed the fact that this Bible of ours is a collection of books. So it is. Now I must stress for you the relationship which exists amongst all these books and the relationship which exists between the Old Testament and the New Testament. Many of the prophecies of the Old Testament, for example, are fulfilled in Our Lord. That fulfillment is recorded in the New Testament. The New Testament, in turn, refers to the Old Testament many times over and makes specific use of many Old Testament prophecies.

The books, while separate, nevertheless, form a continuum, an entire package. One book supports, abets another. You must, therefore, have a good working knowledge of, a good working relationship with, ALL the books of the Bible to grasp fully what God intends, what He is presenting to us in these sacred books.

The Bible is not just history or literature or poetry or a repository of ancient beliefs. Not at all. It is all these things, only incidentally. By means of the vehicle of history or literature or what have you, the main purpose of this book unfolds before our eyes, God's eternal program and the part we are supposed to play in that program.

Essentially the Bible is a "now" book, a timeless book. In a certain sense it belongs to and contains no past or future but only the eternal "now."

I can still recall the example our venerable scripture prof used—Lo! These many years ago!—to explain this concept, especially in relation to the prophetic books of the Bible. "Look at the stars," he would tell us, "with the naked eye. They all look as if they were about the same size. And they are all alive, twinkling in the night sky. Yet we know very well the distances vary considerably, some are close and others are trillions of light years away. Enormous variation exists as to size. And some stars are alive; others are quite dead. The twinkling light we see may well be the light emitted at one time by some star long since burnt out, dead."

So it is with the prophet, with prophetic vision. Many of the events the prophets see are close at hand, others are far distant. But frequently the prophet makes no distinction for he sees the events as occurring without reference to time. But there again, some of the things the prophets did speak of have already occurred (some in this very day and age of ours). We, the present readers, will supply out of our own knowledge an historical framework which may not have been part of the original prophecy. It's just a simple point, but it is an important one. Nor is there a distinction, frequently enough, as to the size or the importance of given events. Many times the prophets speak of future events as you might look at the stars— much the same distance, size, importance and without regard to details of spatial or chronological or historical relationships.

The prophets foretold future events as a God-given office, not simply to forecast the future but, rather, to urge men to turn to God. If men should not turn to God *then*—this or that future punishment would occur. If men do turn to God *then*—this or that future punishment will not occur. Men, as yet, have not turned to God. Therefore certain events (punishments for the sins of mankind) will come to pass.

Too, the prophets foresaw a future redemption and told of a Redeemer who would save us from our sins. Here again, however, much depends on men freely willing to be saved by that Redeemer.

In this sense all of the Bible is prophetic since it looks forward to this one theme—this one master plan, as it were. [In the strict sense, it is estimated that one-third of the Bible is comprised of prophecy.] The viewpoint of the Bible is always forward—and for the one purpose. Our Lord, for example, when answering a question about which commandment of the law is the greatest, said: "You shall love the Lord your God with your whole heart, with your whole soul, and with all your mind. This is the great and first commandment. The second is like it: You shall love your neighbor as yourself. On these two commandments the whole law is based, and the prophets as well" (Mt. 22:34–40).

This quotation, very obviously making use of Deuteronomy, Chapter 6, Verse 4, and Leviticus, Chapter 19, Verse 18, from St. Matthew illustrates the two concepts I have been talking about. One, God's book has but one message: the love of God and the love of neighbor. They are inexorably intertwined and are really one. Two, the Old Testament looks forward to the New Testament; the New Testament fulfills the Old Testament and looks still further forward toward the perfect spiritual life.

The books of the Bible must be viewed as an interdependent whole, their essential unity and union must not be ignored. Seen thus comprehensively, the Bible (all its interrelated books) really does make good sense and proclaims the gospel truth.

There are, of course, many ways of interpreting Sacred Scripture. I think many of you are familiar with some of the applied uses of the Scriptures. In Masses in honor of Our Lady, for example, excerpts taken from the Old Testament Book of Wisdom are used to describe the spiritual relationship which exists between Mary and God. To use these texts thusly to describe Mary is an applied or accommodated use of the text. As long as we realize how the texts are being used this seems quite legitimate.

Too, the Bible is frequently interpreted in an allegorical manner, which has its advantages and disadvantages. However I will talk about that at greater length a bit later. Right now what I really want to take a look at is the literal interpretation of the Bible. When we interpret anything literally we take the words, the sentences, the paragraphs to mean simply what they convey. If the word "cat" is used we take the word "cat" to mean just that—a cat, a four-footed rather furry, aloof beast with claws, and eyes which glow in the dark, and is rather odoriferous, and so forth. [UNLESS, of course, we know from the context that a spiteful woman is meant—in which case the word "cat" means spiteful woman, of course. But all this is really obvious. A stew, for example, is something you eat, except you wouldn't, I think, in Shakespeare's English where the word stew is used quite frequently to mean a brothel. And then consider the difference in meaning of words and phrases in England and in America, as William Buckley, Jr., notes in his *Execution Eve*. P____, F____, K____-__, if you must know—and very wittily, too!]

Thus, we do not go about insisting that the word "cat" really means "dog" because we are more partial to dogs than we are to cats. No. In ordinary usage if the word cat is used then it is a cat that is meant. A cat is a cat is a cat and not a dog. More's the pity, but there it is.

A very real difficulty does exist as far as words are concerned since the Bible was written originally in Hebrew, in Greek, and in Aramaic (a Hebrew dialect). Somewhat later the Bible was translated into Latin and then many centuries after that it was translated into our modern day languages. Therefore the word of caution: when reading an English Bible you are very apt to be reading a translation of a translation of the original text, and with perhaps even another translation or two between you and the original text.

By and large the many translations of the Bible available today are quite good. The few practical norms governing Catholic interpretation of the Bible are an assurance that we are getting at the real meaning of God's word.

Thus:

(1) The inspired writer teaches nothing erroneous.

(2) There is no contradiction amongst the various parts of the Bible.

(3) There is no contradiction between the Bible and certain conclusions of the "profane" sciences.

(4) Any difficulties are to be solved by a deeper, more profound understanding of the Bible, its text, its development, the type of book it is.

(5) Finally, the Bible is to be understood as part of and in the context of total revelation, in the light of the traditions of a living and teaching Church.

Perspective. Now there's a good word, and that's just what is needed for plain ordinary common sense Bible reading. As I have said, there are many ways of reading the Bible. However, I suppose that the literal approach and the symbolistic or allegorical approach are the most common. To view Scripture, or at least great sections of Scripture, in an allegorical way is quite popular today, as it was many centuries ago.

As you know, an allegory is a prolonged metaphor, wherein a series of actions is symbolic of other actions. Now, as you know very well, the Bible can be read and understood in a literal sense; but the Bible can also be read and understood in a figurative sense.

To read the Scriptures in a figurative sense is to place emphasis on what is called the secondary and yet more spiritual, more profound sense. To interpret Scripture in such a way may be nice but it can also be rather dangerous and lead you astray. It is true, however, that Scripture was interpreted in this way as far back as Origen and Augustine. For example, Augustine thought that many of the prophecies in the Bible concerning the latter days should be understood in a *symbolic* way, finding *symbolic* fulfillment in this the Church age. Yet now—many centuries later—we are seeing many of these very same prophecies being fulfilled *literally*, before our very eyes.

By the same token you cannot read the Scriptures uncritically, accepting each and every statement literally. When Our Lord says, "If your right eye offend you, pluck it out!" He is not telling you to gouge out your eye literally. What He *is* saying, in a dramatic and figurative way, is to avoid anything that might cause you to lose heaven and to be cast into hell.

There exists a norm for interpreting Scripture called by some the Golden Rule which makes very good sense:

"When the plain sense of Scripture makes common sense, seek no other sense; therefore, take every word at its primary, ordinary, usual, literal meaning unless the facts of the immediate context, studied in the light of related passages and axiomatic and fundamental truths, indicate clearly otherwise." (See Pentecost, *Things to Come*, p. 42.)

I think that is about the briefest, most common sense approach to the reading of Scripture you'll ever see.

As for prophecy in particular, some problems exist. Some of the problems exist because the prophets persist in prophesying on *their* own terms. We who read or listen to the prophets persist in reading or listening on *our* own terms. In a word, of course, the problem is communication.

Yet it is easy enough to avoid many of the problems traditionally associated with the prophetic Scriptures. The prophetic Scriptures possess certain characteristics and these characteristics should be used to reduce problems to a minimum. Thus: granted the revelation to the prophets, the future was seen by them as either immediately present, complete, or with all the events in progress (as if everything was happening at the same time); prophecy may appear as just one event when, in fact, there may be a two or three or even four-fold fulfillment; prophecy is sometimes presented through a great number of individual facts (which may, at times, even seem contradictory). A good example: the prophecies which saw Our Lord in His glory and also as the Suffering Servant. As we now know, both prophetic portraits were and are true. Too, some prophecies are conditional. For example Our Lord uses the prophecies of Jonah to show that God's wrath can be averted if prophecy is heeded. Another most important fact which you must keep in mind: the prophets spoke of future events in terms of, the context of, the language of their own society and experience.

And I think I have already mentioned the fact that the prophets often speak of the future as if it were the present, they sometimes speak of the future as if it were past, and they often see a whole series of variously timed events as if they were happening all at the same time. You already know about this problem of the time element in the prophetic Scriptures, so let's press on to another problem.

That next problem: the law of double reference. The prophets usually had a message for their own times as well as a message for some future time. The same prophecy can have a double meaning. (No! Not double-entendre. Usually, that is!) Two widely separated events are often brought together in the one prophecy. One and the same prophecy can refer to two different events, one near, the other far distant. As you can readily see, this can cause a bit of difficulty when reading prophecy. Often enough, to get at the meaning of the prophets and their prophecies you have to read with sense and sensibility, to say nothing of just a bare minimum of careful study.

Prophets can speak to us in diverse ways. They may quite simply proclaim their prophecies in a straightforward, uncomplicated manner. Then, again, they may make their prophecies known through types, through symbols, through parables. Too, prophetic revelations can be received by means of dreams and ecstasies. All these things must be kept in mind, at the tip of your fingers, as it were, and ready for use as you are reading the prophetic Scriptures.

Types. In the Old Testament there exist persons, places, and things which in some manner pre-figure, and, therefore, have a corresponding relationship to certain persons, places, and things of the New Testament. According to the common usage which has developed over the years and centuries this preordained relationship is described by the words *type* and *anti-type*. Granted a corresponding relationship, the persons or places or things in the Old Testament are labeled the type; the persons or places or things of the New Testament are called or labeled the anti-type.

Keep in mind that the types of the Old Testament had a valid, independent, historical existence of their own. Moreover, at the precise historical moment when the type existed, no one may have at all realized the further signification for a later era (the Christian era, that is). An example: Our Lord uses the example of the Brazen Serpent in Exodus as a type of His own death. He would be lifted up for the salvation of mankind. The Brazen Serpent was the type; Our Crucified Lord was the anti-type. The type is prophetic in that it does prefigure a future and corresponding anti-type. However, it is also true that the prefiguring relationship of the Old Testament frequently will not be known or understood until it has been made manifest, especially by the events of Our Lord's life, and has been recorded in the pages of the New Testament. But then the relationship is made unmistakably clear.

Symbols. Six kinds of symbols may be listed which are of a prophetic nature: persons, institutions, offices, events, actions, things. These matters must be handled most cautiously and with sound guidance, as I am sure you understand. The following three rules for handling symbols seem good: names of symbols are to be understood in a literal sense; symbols always denote something essentially different from themselves; some slight, small resemblance between the symbol and the thing symbolized can be seen.

In any case, when dealing with Bible prophecy, symbols which are used are also explained almost immediately. The meaning usually is clear. Furthermore the symbols used in the Apocalypse are to be found, in germ, at least, and for the most part, in Isaiah, Ezekiel, Daniel, or Zechariah.

Parables. Parables, as you well know, are the wise sayings or the fictitious short stories used by Our Lord to set forth His teachings. We would merely note, at the present moment, that some of the details of the Parousia, the Latter Days, are to be gleaned from a number of parables used by Our Lord. Some examples include the parable of the talents, the parable of the five wise and the five foolish virgins, the parable of the separation of the sheep and the goats.

As for prophetic revelation through dreams and ecstasies, you are familiar with this concept. All of you know of the revelations made to Saint Joseph, for example, concerning Our Blessed Lady and also Our Lord, revelations made known by means of dreams.

Briefly, then, and to re-cap, these are the norms which will guide us as we read and interpret prophecy. Look for a *literal* interpretation. Some literal truth is being revealed, regardless of form; the overall *harmony* of the entire prophetic program must be borne in mind. No prophecy stands by itself; consider carefully the *perspective* and the *time relationship* of prophecy. Prophecy is to be interpreted *Christologically.* Our Lord is at the center of all prophecy; know the *historical context* of prophecy, of course. Apply the *law of double reference.* Finally, *be consistent.*

These norms, rules, regulations or whatever you wish to call them must be part of your background, that knowledge you bring *to* the prophetic Scriptures if you are going to read these same Scriptures with understanding and profit.

Do not put words in the prophet's mouth, thus having him utter that which, in reality, he never said at all. By the same token do not take words out of the prophet's mouth, thus vitiating or even destroying the sense of what the prophet was trying to convey.

To my mind, it is really extremely important to keep constantly in the forefront of your mind, the Bible you are reading is most probably a translation of a translation of a translation. I have said that before, I know. I may say it again later on. But you should understand that you are not reading a literal word-for-word translation of the original Bible. Admittedly, such a thing is impossible. Many words and phrases in one language do not admit of a translation into another language. Exactly the same problem arises when you try to translate poetry from one language into another. It simply doesn't translate.

Try translating the following famous English limerick into German.

> There was a young fellow named Hall
> Who fell in the spring in the fall.
> 'Twould have been a sad thing
> Had he died in the spring,
> But he didn't—he died in the fall.

It cannot be done without losing the entire play on the English words spring and fall and thus the humorous point of the limerick itself. But to get back to the Bible, often what you are reading are paraphrases of the original text whereby the translator strives to convey the *sense* of the original text. But this—most unfortunately—means that at times we are reading the sense of the original text—as the translator conceives it to be!

A word to the wise should suffice.

While it is true, as we have already pointed out, that there is about the Bible as a whole a certain prophetic aura, presenting as it does salvation history, three principal themes dominate Bible prophecy. These themes are (1) the Nations, (2) the Jews, (3) the Church (and the Kingdom). While all the prophetic books and texts of the Bible deal with one or another or all of these three themes, the books of Daniel, of Ezekiel, of Revelation treat of them in much detail. The prophetic book of Daniel deals with the Nations; Ezekiel's prophecies concern the Jews, primarily; the book of Revelation focuses, primarily, on the Church and the Kingdom. It is these books which supply us with the skeleton, the framework, upon which we are able to build, to flesh out the picture painted by the prophetic Scriptures.

The prophetic books of the Old Testament are generally grouped in two sections: (1) books which treat of their own times and the future; (2) books which treat only of the future. As for the New Testament, the book of Revelation is *the* book of prophetic Scripture. Prophetic texts abound, however, in the other books of the New Testament, and especially in St. Paul. Indeed, thirty-eight books of the Bible contain references to the latter days.

Those books of the Old Testament which treat of current and future events are: Isaiah, Jeremiah, Ezekiel, Daniel, Hosea, Amos, Micah, Zephaniah, Haggai, Zechariah. Those which deal with future events, rather than of events current to their own times, are: Joel, Obadiah, Nahum, Habakkuk, Malachi.

Such knowledge helps you to get at the Bbile's meaning. An understanding of certain phrases is also helpful. The use of the phrase *"In that day"* lets us know that the prophet is at the beginning of a new or another subject and, moreover, subjects, events having to do with *"The Day of the Lord."* Other such phrases are: the last days, the latter days, the end, the time of the end, the end-times, the end of the world (age), at that time. There are some other variations, but the listing I have just given you should provide you with more than enough clues in determining when the prophet is speaking of the events that will occur at the end of this present Church age.

Another hint: always be aware of, alert to, the goal of the Bible's author. Redemption is the key word. St. Paul says: "Behold: all things are made new." St. John states: "I saw a new heaven and a new earth, for the first heaven and the first earth were passed away." Then Our Lord will reign in Glory over the people, places, things He redeemed and has caused to become new. And that is what prophecy is all about: the restoration of all things in Christ.

Part II
The New and Everlasting Covenant

The restoration of all things in Christ is God's new covenant with all mankind. We say, in the most sacred part of the Mass, the moment of consecration:

Take this, all of you, and drink from it. This is the cup of my blood, the blood of the NEW AND EVERLASTING COVENANT. It will be shed for you and for all men so that sins may be forgiven. Do this in memory of me.

Prior to this covenant of the New Testament there existed, obviously, covenants of the Old Testament, binding and eternal covenants, established by God with men.

These covenants were (and are) unconditional or conditional. Through them God deigns to bind Himself in grace to a contractual obligation, to fulfill that which He promises or agrees to for the covenanted ones. These promises are made either without any reservations or they may be dependent upon certain given conditions. In any case, a contract, a most solemn agreement, is entered upon by God freely with His chosen ones. Should the contract, the agreement, be conditional then God's promise of fulfillment is based upon the fulfillment of or the failure to fulfill the conditions, the promise of special blessings if the conditions are fulfilled, of punishment if the conditions are not fulfilled.

These covenants are real (that is, literal), they are eternal, and made with a covenant people (Israel). The four great covenants that God made with Israel are: the Abrahamic covenant, the Palestinian covenant, the Davidic covenant, and the New covenant of the Old Testament. The basis for all these covenants and, indeed, for the entire covenant program is the Abrahamic covenant.

In Genesis 12:1–3, God said to Abram, "Leave your country, your family, and your father's house, for the land I will show you. I will make you a great nation; I will bless you and make your name so famous that it will be used as a blessing.

"I will bless those who bless you. I will curse those who curse you. All the tribes of the earth shall bless themselves by you." JB

And in Genesis 15:18–19, God promised Abraham:

To your descendants I give land, from the Wadi of Egypt, to the Great River, the river Euphrates . . .

It is abundantly clear, then, from what we have just said that, by reason of the Abrahamic covenant, Israel possesses the title deed to the land of Palestine. Since the one condition to the promise was fulfilled by Abraham when he left the land of Ur, Ur of the Chaldees, and traveled to a strange land, the eschatological implications are clear. This covenant will be fulfilled and is being fulfilled in our own day.

At a later time, and at a time of crisis, when it fell to Joshua to lead the Israelites into the land promised to Abraham, God reaffirmed the original covenant. Israel was to possess this land; this land is Israel's inheritance. Thus, in Deuteronomy 30:1–10, we read as follows:

"And when all these things come upon you, the blessing and the curse, which I have set before you, and you call them to mind among all the nations where the LORD your God has driven you, and return to the LORD your God, you and your children, and obey his voice in all that I command you this day, with all your heart and with all your soul; then the LORD your God will restore your fortunes, and have compassion upon you, and he will gather you again from all the peoples where the LORD your God has scattered you. If your outcasts are in the uttermost parts of heaven, from there the LORD your God will gather you, and from there he will fetch you; and the LORD your God will bring you into the land which your fathers possessed, that you may possess it; and he will make you more prosperous and numerous than your fathers. And the LORD your God will circumcise your heart and the heart of your offspring, so that you will love the LORD your God with all your heart and with all your soul, that you may live. And the LORD your God will put all these curses upon your foes and enemies who persecuted you. And you shall again obey the voice of the LORD, and keep all his commandments which I command you this day. The LORD your God will make you abundantly prosperous in all the work of your hand, in the fruit of your body, and in the fruit of your cattle, and in the fruit of your ground; for the LORD will again take delight in prospering you, as he took delight in your fathers, if you obey the voice of the LORD your God, to keep his commandments and his statutes which are written in this book of the law, if you turn to the LORD your God with all your heart and with all your soul." RSV

As you yourselves can see at once, several things are clear. The Israelite nation has been taken from the land of the promise. (This because of their unfaithfulness.) The Israelites will repent, however. The nation will be restored to the land and Israel, as a nation, will be converted. Israel's relation to the land is a matter of the utmost importance, obviously. God absolutely guarantees the nation Israel the possession of the land.

For example, in Ezekiel 16:60–62, the Lord once again affirms this Palestinian covenant. Just take a look at what the Lord has to say:

". . . I will remember my covenant with you in the days of your youth, and I will establish with you an *everlasting* covenant."

Despite Israel's unfaithfulness and disobedience, the persistent falling away in disbelief, the land of the promise remained and would continue to be always—the land of the promise. "God never takes back His gifts or revokes His choice" (Rom. 11:29).

The covenant is to be fulfilled literally. It is unconditional, save for the condition of time. The complete fulfillment of this covenant (which is but an amplification and enlargement of sections of the Abrahamic covenant) will occur at that time when Israel as a nation is converted.

The first part of the covenant is being fulfilled right now, at the very moment that I am writing these words on paper.

God promised Abraham that he would possess the land and that *this land* would belong not only to him but to his descendants. Furthermore God promised Abraham that his *seed* would possess the land eternally. In the Davidic covenant God enlarges upon and confirms His promises concerning the seed of Abraham. Thus: in 2 Samuel 7:12–16: "And when your time comes and you rest with your ancestors, I will raise up your heir after you, sprung from your loins, and I will make his kingdom firm. It is he who shall build a house for my name. And I will make his royal throne firm forever. I will be a father to him, and he shall be a son to me. And if he does wrong, I will correct him with the rod of men and human chastisements; but I will not withdraw my favor from him as I withdrew it from your predecessor Saul, whom I removed from my presence. Your house and your kingdom shall endure forever before me; your throne shall stand firm forever."

You are reading along in your Bible, I know, as we go along citing all these prophetic texts. Therefore I don't have to supply the context of all the quotations I have used or will be using. That you can do yourselves just as well as I can; indeed, better, for all I know. Therefore, all I need say about the quotation from 2 Samuel is that: (1) God promises David that he will have a child who will succeed him and establish his kingdom; (2) this son will build the Temple as God's dwelling place (the famous temple of Solomon); (3) the throne of the kingdom will be established forever (even though some of the things Solomon would do should merit such a punishment as loss of the throne); (4) David's *house, throne,* and *kingdom* are to be forever.

You can see for yourselves that no conditions are attached to God's promise. And, once again, the covenant is to be interpreted quite literally. Apply your common sense. Portions of the promise have been fulfilled—and literally. Therefore the parts of the promise yet to be fulfilled will be fulfilled in the same way—literally.

So—I repeat the situation once again. There exists the matter of current events, the historical occurrences of our own times. The latter portions of the promise are being fulfilled in our own times. So—apply your common sense.

(1) Israel has been preserved as a nation.

(2) Israel is being brought back to the land of the promise, David's kingdom.

Therefore it will follow: that Our Lord will return to the earth, bodily, literally, to reign over David's kingdom; David's kingdom will, therefore, be re-established, an earthly kingdom, literally; this kingdom will be eternal.

Like it or not, believe it or not, these events will come to be. We have God's most solemn promise on it.

There is yet another covenant which God has made with Israel— the fourth great determinative covenant. It is this covenant which promises guarantees that Israel will know a conversion which will be the foundation of all future blessings.

So, in Jeremiah 31:31–34, we read:

"Behold, the days are coming, says the LORD, when I will make a new covenant with the house of Israel and the house of Judah, not like the covenant which I made with their fathers when I took them by the hand to bring them out of the land of Egypt, my covenant which they broke, though I was their husband, says the LORD. But this is the covenant which I will make with the house of Israel after those days, says the LORD: I will put my law within them, and I will write it upon their hearts; and I will be their God, and they shall be my people. And no longer shall each man teach his neighbor and each his brother, saying, 'Know the LORD,' for they shall all know me, from the least of them to the greatest, says the LORD; for I will forgive their iniquity, and I will remember their sin no more." RSV

This new covenant, then, is unconditional and eternal. It promises regeneration of mind and heart and God's blessing. It certainly implies the indwelling of the Holy Spirit.

And how are we to regard this new covenant? Unless we understand it in its literal sense and look for a literal fulfillment, we make a mockery of Sacred Scripture and its Author. It is eternal, it depends on the will of God, it is the amplification of the blessings of the Abrahamic covenant.

These are the elements of its fulfillment: Israel must first be regathered and thence restored to the land. Then Israel will know God's blessings, as promised. It also seems clear that blessings follow upon Israel's conversion. This conversion follows upon the return of Our Lord. These blessings will, so it seems, be granted in the millennial age.

Of course, it has often been argued (and I feel sure you have heard this in many a sermon) that these covenants, and most especially the New Covenant of the Old Testament, have been and are being fulfilled by the Church. Certainly it is true that Our Lord, by shedding His blood on the cross for all mankind, established a new and eternal covenant. In this new covenant of the New Testament all—including the nation Israel—are saved. But the original covenant—the Abrahamic covenant—remains and maintains its full force. Since the New Covenant spoken of in Jeremiah is the reaffirmation of the blessings of the Abrahamic covenant, this New Covenant of the Old Testament will be fulfilled—but with the nation Israel. I suppose you could say that it receives its efficacy and effectiveness from the salvific covenant founded on the blood of Our Lord.

In any event, the time of the beginnings of its fulfillment—as was the case with the other three covenants we have considered—is now. It may be, indeed, that the millennial age is at hand.

We have mentioned several times now the future conversion of Israel. This means, as you probably have already surmised, a conversion to Our Lord. This will happen in its proper time according to the overall prophetic plan God has graciously revealed to us. Even as the promise, the prophecies of the Old Testament about the Messiah—Our Lord—have been fulfilled, and fulfilled literally at that, so also the promise, the prophecies of the Old Testament about the nation Israel will be fulfilled. For example, Ezekiel tells us that Israel will be brought back to the land as *one* nation, not as *two* nations (Israel and Judah). You can see this for yourself by simply looking it up in Ezekiel, Chapter 37, Verses 15-23.

THE NEW AND EVERLASTING COVENANT

Let us stop, for just a moment, and take a look at some of the Old Testament prophecies which refer to Our Lord. St. Matthew traces Our Lord's family history back to David, thus showing that Our Lord is "the son of David." This is one of the most common of the messianic titles. Our Lord Himself quotes Psalm 110:

The Lord said unto my Lord: Sit at my right hand while I make your enemies your footstool (Mt. 22:44).

Whereby Our Lord avers that, not only is He descended from David, His origins are also Divine.

Our Lord was born of the Virgin Mary, as you know. And, again, you know that this fact is a fulfillment of Isaiah's prophecy:

The virgin shall be with child and give birth to a son, and they shall call him Emmanuel (Is. 7:10–14).

The Messiah was to be born in Bethlehem, in the land of Judah. The prophet Micah proclaimed:

"But you, O Bethlehem Ephrathah, who are too small to be among the clans of Judah, from you shall come forth for me one who is to be ruler in Israel, whose origin is from of old, from ancient days" (Mi. 5:1–2; Mt. 2:6). This prophecy, referring as it does to the Messiah's human origins and to His eternal origins, is applied by St. Matthew to Our Lord who was, indeed, born in Bethlehem of the land of Judah, and whose eternal origins can hardly be gainsaid.

St. Matthew is well able to say of Our Lord that it was He of whom Hosea spoke when the prophet said: "Out of Egypt I have called my son" (Hos. 11:1; Mt. 2:15). You know that Gospel as well as I do. I do not have to repeat it here. You are familiar with the many prophecies of Isaiah which refer to Our Lord. And, as you know very well, St. Matthew does just that. Just two examples: A herald would announce the Lord's coming. So St. John the Baptist announced Our Lord's coming, even as Isaiah said:

A herald's voice in the desert: Prepare the way of the Lord, make straight his paths (Mt. 3:3; Is. 40:3).

And:
Our Lord left Nazareth to live in Capernaum, even as Isaiah said:

Land of Zebulon, land of Naphtali along the sea beyond the Jordan, heathen Galilee. A people living in darkness has seen a great light. On those who inhabit a land overshadowed by death, light has arisen (Is. 9:1; Mt. 4:15–16).

Of the Messiah's ministry, Isaiah says, for example: "Behold your God will come with vengeance, with the recompense of God. He will come and save you.

"Then the eyes of the blind shall be opened, and the ears of the deaf unstopped; then shall the lame man leap like a hart and the tongue of the dumb sing for joy" (Is. 35:4–6).

Our Lord quotes these very words in answer to the question of John the Baptist: "Are you 'He who is to come' or do we look for another?" Jesus' answer: "Go back and report to John what you hear and see: the blind recover their sight, cripples walk, lepers are cured, the deaf hear, dead men are raised to life and the poor have the good news preached to them" (Mt. 11:2–6). Our Lord applied this prophecy of the Messiah to Himself, substantiating His claim by the miracles He was performing.

He taught in parables, even as Isaiah said He would. In the words of Psalm 78:2, Our Lord would:

. . . open my mouth in a parable; I will utter dark sayings from of old . . . (See Mt. 13:34.)

The people would pay homage to Our Lord but their hearts would be far from Him, even as the prophet said. And surely Our Lord was the stone which the builders rejected, who became the keystone of the structure, the structure of faith and salvation, as the prophet foretold. The list could continue. You could add yet other prophecies fulfilled in Our Lord which I have passed over.

Our Lord used the title "Son of Man" of Himself many times and here, once again, we have a messianic title. In Ezekiel, of course, the title is used to express the lowly human condition:

"Such was the appearance of the likeness of the glory of the Lord. And when I saw it, I fell upon my face. And I heard the voice of one speaking. And he said to me, 'O son of man, stand upon your feet, and I will speak with you' " (Ezek. 1:1–2).

This phrase also denotes glory and divine overlordship. Thus, in Daniel, we see:

As the visions during the night continued, I saw One like a Son of Man coming, on the clouds of heaven; when he reached the Ancient One and was presented before him, He received dominion, glory, and kingship; nations and peoples of every language serve him. His dominion is an ever-lasting dominion that shall not be taken away, his kingship shall not be destroyed (Dan. 7:13–14).

Our Lord applies this title to Himself:

"Then the sign of the Son of Man will appear in the sky and 'all the clans of earth will strike their breasts' as they see 'the Son of Man coming in the clouds of heaven' with power and great glory" (Mt. 24:30).

I suppose the prophecies of Isaiah which describe the suffering Messiah are familiar to most of us. These prophecies are used extensively in the liturgy of Holy Week, the one time most of us do manage to get to church (on Palm Sunday and Easter Sunday, at any rate!).

Isaiah depicts one who is a suffering servant, a servant who is himself sinless, one who will save his people from their sins. His appearance would be so maimed as to be beyond human semblance, his form beyond that of the sons of men. Yet because of this he will be exalted. Many nations shall be startled by him and, thence, begin to grasp the meaning of the suffering servant.

He would possess no comeliness, no beauty to attract us. He would be a man of grief, a man familiar with sorrow. Therefore there will be those of us who will turn from him, despise him.

You know, just as well as I do, that these prophetic utterances were literally fulfilled by the manner of Our Lord's death.

(I might add a thought here about the reading of prophecy. If you are referring to Isaiah 52:13–53:12 as you are reading this—and I surely hope you are—you will notice that Isaiah writes of all these events in the *past* tense. This is a common literary device. When the writer wished to denote the certainty of the prophecy, he would write in this past tense. In Hebrew this is called the prophetic perfect.)

In any case, to return to our Suffering Servant. He would bear *our* griefs, carry *our* sorrows, he would be wounded for *our* transgressions. Yet we are healed by means of his punishments. The Lord laid upon him *our* inequities. He would be as a lamb led to slaughter, and would not open his mouth in protest. He would be cut off—that is, killed—from the living, his grave would be with the wicked, he would be with a rich man in his death.

Again, what can I say? You know very well that all these oracles were perfectly and literally fulfilled in Our Lord.

Let us turn now to the prophet Zechariah. Speaking of the shepherd to be slain, the prophet says: "Then I said to them, 'If it seems right to you, give me my wages; but if not, keep them.' And they weighed out as my wages thirty shekels of silver. Then the Lord said to me, 'Cast it into the treasury—the lordly price at which I was paid off by them.' So I took the thirty shekels of silver and cast them into the treasury in the house of the Lord" (Zech. 11:12–13). Needless to say, Judas did not mark his price down to 29.95.

Consider now Psalm 22. The very first words of that Psalm, "My God, my God, why hast thou forsaken me?" are the words Our Lord uses in His death agony as He hangs upon the cross. As the psalmist continues, Our Lord is described as a worm and no man, scorned by men and mocked at. The people wag their heads at him and say, "Let the Lord rescue him!"

The death agony of a crucified man can hardly be more vividly portrayed:

I am poured out like water, and all my bones are out of joint; my heart is like wax, it is melted within my breast; my strength is dried up like a pot-sherd, and my tongue cleaves to my jaws. RSV

Then, phrases many of you know by heart:

They have pierced my hands and feet; I can count all my bones. They stare and gloat over me; they divide my garments among them, and for my raiment they cast lots. RSV

Each of these prophetic utterances has been perfectly AND LITERALLY fulfilled in Our Lord.

I need say no more.

Since these prophecies relating to Our Lord have been fulfilled, we may quite seriously and legitimately look to the fulfillment of the rest of the prophecies concerning Our Lord.

Since the prophecies relating to Israel's return to the land are being fulfilled, we may quite seriously and legitimately look to the fulfillment of the rest of the prophecies concerning Israel.

It is by way of an aside, I suppose, but one aspect of Israel's return to the land fascinates me: the part the United States played in this drama. One part of that drama involved Harry Truman, then President of the United States. The hows and whys and wherefores of his participation will always be the subject of historical doubt, I suppose, historical truth being what it is. What does seem clear is a fascinating bit of history.

So far as I can understand it, at one point in the year 1948, Truman was quite bitter about attacks made upon him by some over-zealous Zionists. Apparently he was not going to support the partition of Palestine into an Arab and a Jewish state, a United Nations resolution about to be voted upon by the General Assembly of that body. So resentful was he of the intense political pressure being exerted upon him by American Jewish leaders that he finally refused to see them or meet with them in any way. He even refused to see Chaim Weizman. And without United States support the resolution stood no chance of winning approval at the United Nations.

Now, this is the bit of history that really intrigues me. One Jewish-American had access to President Truman. That man was Eddie Jacobson, a friend and a former business partner in that famous haberdashery venture which failed in the recession of 1922. Jacobson did get to see Truman. It would seem (according to several books on the subject) that Jacobson did persuade Truman to see Chaim Weizman, founding father of the Jewish state, Israel. Certainly Mr. Truman did pledge United States support for the partition of Palestine and the nation of Israel. Certainly it is true that very shortly after its establishment, President Truman announced American recognition of the Jewish state, Israel.

I don't know how historians will evaluate that bit of history. Evidently the government of Israel thought it highly significant since, among the many commemorative stamps I am sure they have issued, one commemorates an American President, Harry Truman.

May 14, 1948, was, indeed, a turning point in the history of the Holy Land. The Jewish people had now a state, a nation, a land after almost two thousand years of exile. Dispersed, scattered throughout the world by the Romans following the destruction of Jerusalem in the year A.D. 70, the Jews were now able to return to the land of the promise.

It is quite impossible to set down in a few sentences the well-nigh innumerable events which preceded, in some way led up to *the* major historical event of the present century. (I know this century has been a century of major events. I know that man did land on the moon! Time will bear me out, however. *The* major event of this century *will be* the return of the Jewish people to the land of the promise.)

It was Theodore Herzl who, in the latter years of the 1890's, certainly inspired and was a founder of the Zionist movement. He it was who proposed a Jewish state in Palestine. Other great Jewish leaders were part of the Zionist movement, men such as David Green who changed his name to David Ben-Gurion. It was to him and to fellow Zionists, to Chaim Weizman, that the British gave the Balfour Declaration. This declaration of Nov. 2, 1917, recognized the historic rights of the Jewish people in Palestine.

Only after World War II did the Jews return to Palestine in great numbers. Now in 1948, having governed the land for some thirty years, the British were leaving. It was at this point that the United Nations, under extraordinary pressure from the United States to grant approval, did give its approval to a new (or reborn) Jewish state, Israel. And it was in June of 1967 that the Nation Israel regained, controlled, made its own the Holy City Jerusalem. Just where that will lead us remains to be seen.

Given the momentous events which we have just listed for you, it would seem opportune to pick up your Bible and start to read it, start to meditate on its words. Keep in mind, please, those basic rules we have touched on so briefly. They will, if you apply them, help you to understand this book of books which is, as it is said, ever old and ever new.

We have opted for a literal approach to Bible prophecy. The momentous occurrences of our times seem to cry out for such an interpretation. But bear in mind that not every single word in the Bible is to be so interpreted. Use common sense. Apply the Golden Rule. As the Second Vatican Council points out in its Dogmatic Constitution on Divine Revelation (Dei Verbum) God has chosen to speak to us in the Sacred Scriptures through men in human fashion:

"Those who search out the intention of the sacred writers must, among other things, have regard for 'literary forms.' For truth is proposed and expressed in a variety of ways, depending on whether a text is history of one kind or another, or whether its form is that of prophecy, poetry, or some other type of speech. The interpreter must investigate what meaning the sacred writer intended to express and actually expressed in particular circumstances as he used contemporary literary forms in accordance with the situation of his own time and culture. For the correct understanding of what the sacred author wanted to assert, due attention must be paid to the customary and characteristic styles of perceiving, speaking, and narrating which prevailed at the time of the sacred writer, and to the customs men normally followed at that period in their everyday dealings with one another." (The Documents of Vatican II, Dogmatic Constitution on Divine Revelation, Chapter III, Section 11.)

Over and above a formal and academic, albeit fascinating, approach to the Sacred Scriptures, we ourselves should flesh out the bare bones of the written word by our reflexive, meditative reading of this holy book. The written word thence becomes the Living Word.

Pope Pius XII, in his Encyclical "Divino Afflante Spiritu," quotes St. Jerome thusly: " 'To ignore the Scriptures is to ignore Christ . . . . If there is anything which sustains the wise man in times of strife and amid disasters and upheavals in the world, anything which helps him to remain steadfast in serenity of mind, it is, in the first place, I consider, meditation on the Scriptures and knowledge of them.' "

III

Signs of the Times

The events of the latter days can be separated into seven basic and chronological divisions. To divide historical events into strict chronological sections is unrealistic, as you well know. Events overlap one another and, in reality, no such clear division exists. On the other hand a simplified, chronological division does make it a bit easier to remember the important events of any given era and to remember (within reason) the time sequence. And, therefore, since renowned, world-famous historians do this very thing, I think I will too, not that I am renowned or world-famous, but I am writing a history of the latter days for you.

Those seven chronological steps, then: (1) the events preceding the Rapture, (2) the Rapture, (3) the persecution of the Church, (4) the Russian invasion of Israel, (5) the five plagues, (6) Armageddon, (7) the Second Coming.

Now as it happens (and this is the only time it does happen, you may believe!) the very first topic, the events preceding the Rapture, fall quite nicely into seven topics. Since that happens to be the case, I will simply list these topics for you and we can discuss each one of them in turn. (So it is the easy, almost lazy way of discussing these topics. What's wrong with that? I'm in favor of doing things the easiest way possible.) In any case these seven topics are: (1) false Christs, wars, rumors of wars, commotions, famine, plague and earthquakes; (2) the destruction of the temple, the need for a new temple; (3) the return of the Jews (some of them, that is) to the Holy Land; (4) the apostasy; (5) the ten nation federation; (6) the great leader (the anti-Christ); (7) the time of peace and security, which *follows* upon the time of wars and rumors of war.

If we just take each of these topics step by step we'll all acquire a reasonably clear picture of the end-time, the latter days, the day of the Lord.

The first topic is: false Christs, wars, rumors of wars, commotions, famine, plague, earthquakes. We can find this topic discussed at some length by St. Matthew in his 24th chapter. Our Lord and His disciples had gathered at the Mount of Olives. Our Lord was seated. The disciples were asking Our Lord about the signs of His coming and also of the end of the world. So Our Lord told them that they should take care that no one lead them astray. He said, "Be on guard! Many will come attempting to impersonate me. 'I am the Messiah!' they will claim, and they will deceive many. You will hear of wars and rumors of wars" (Mt. 24:1–6).

Now, I can hear you muttering to yourselves, "What kind of sign is that? We've had wars and rumors of wars since the year One!" But bear in mind that Our Lord was speaking to a Jewish audience and primarily only about the *land of Israel.* There were no Jews on the land, once the Romans got through with them, and, indeed, no land of Israel around to hear about these wars and rumors of war *prior to these our present days.*

True enough. The important point that must be considered with the utmost care and seriousness is: NOW, IN OUR TIMES, ALL THE VARIOUS SIGNS MENTIONED IN THE BIBLE (THE OLD TESTAMENT AND THE NEW TESTAMENT) CONCERNING THE LATTER DAYS ARE OCCURRING AT THE SAME TIME, WITHIN THE SAME TIME PERIOD. THIS HAS NEVER HAPPENED BEFORE.

And therein lies the precise point of this book. To continue, therefore, with these signs of the latter days. Wars and rumors of wars. A glance through any of our daily newspapers or weekly news magazines should be sufficient evidence that wars and rumors of wars are quite ordinary, quite the usual thing at present. This is true for almost all parts of the world *and* it is certainly true at present in the Holy Land.

Our Lord also mentioned the fact that false Messiahs would appear, men saying, "I am the Messiah." Now, here again, you can make the objection that over the centuries, both before and after Our Lord's death and resurrection, there have been men who have claimed to be the messiah. There is no question that this is absolutely true. *And* it is true *now.* I have no intention of mentioning any names or sects. (Maybe I'll insert a footnote!) In any case, you know very well, that just here in the United States there exist a number of persons who claim (directly or indirectly) to be the messiah and they are deceiving many. (Latest figures indicate that these sects can claim well over three million followers, mostly young people. And this is just in the United States.) Again, this is easily verifiable by perusing copies of any of our larger daily or Sunday newspapers or weekly news magazines.

I would ask you to please keep in mind that we are discussing only those signs we consider as preliminary to the Rapture. There exists always the difficulty of separating the signs preliminary to the actual event of Our Lord's Second Coming. Some of the signs are rather the same. Therefore it is most important that you understand and grasp the fact that the Rapture occurs about ten and a half years before the Second Coming. The two events are obviously related but they are, nevertheless, separated by ten and one-half years. Indeed, there are some signs which occur before the Rapture and continue after the Rapture but with a far greater intensity. Our Lord Himself said:

"Do not be alarmed. Such things are bound to happen, BUT THAT IS NOT YET THE END. Nation will rise against nation, one kingdom against another. There will be famine and pestilence and earthquakes in many places. THESE ARE THE EARLY STAGES OF THE BIRTH PANGS" (Mt. 24:6–8).

Birth pangs, the labor pains which are part of the process of giving birth occur, at first, somewhat infrequently. Then, of course, as the time of birth nears, those labor pains become much more frequent. Then they occur at regular and frequent intervals. These, in turn, lead up to the actual moment of birth and the pain associated with the giving of birth.

Our Lord, then, gave us a very fundamental and graphic analogy to describe the time of the latter days and, finally, the actual moment of the Second Coming. The wars, the rumors of wars, the famine (which is going on all over the third world), the earthquakes (going on all around the globe), which I am sure you know just from an ordinary perusal of the newspapers, the false messiahs preaching a false doctrine, and the other calamities mentioned are the birth pangs. These will occur, at first, rather infrequently. But, then, as the time of the Second Coming nears, they will start to happen at regular and frequent intervals leading up to the final events, the birth pangs to be associated with the actual moment of the Second Coming.

Obviously the birth pangs are coming at more frequent and regular intervals. Again, obviously, those intervals between the birth pangs, the signs, do exist. It would seem, moreover, as of the moment, that the intervals between calamities are getting shorter, more frequent. For example, the years of peace between Israeli wars are getting shorter. Apparently the pain of the moment of birth is really *beginning* to *take over*.

Before turning to a couple of prophecies from the Old Testament concerning the signs which are preliminary to the Rapture of the Church, I would like to stress these words of Our Lord:

"From the fig tree learn a lesson. When its branch grows tender and sprouts leaves, you realize that summer is near. Likewise, when you see all these things happening, you will know that he is near, standing at the door. I ASSURE YOU, THE PRESENT GENERATION WILL NOT PASS AWAY UNTIL ALL THIS TAKES PLACE . . ." (Mt. 24:32–34).

Do you realize that the fig tree is a symbol of Israel? For example, in St. Mark's gospel, Chapter 11, Verses 12 and 20, Our Lord curses a fig tree because it is bearing no fruit. (The symbol involved: Our Lord curses Israel for bearing no fruit.) Then, as the Greek version brings out, the fig tree withers, down to—but not including the roots. (The symbol involved: the cursed and withered fig tree will live again.)

Apply the symbol to Our Lord's description of the end-times. When the fig tree starts to bud know that summer is near (Lk. 21:29). (The symbol involved: when Israel starts to live again, the end-times are near.)

At the very least, all that is an eye-opening thought.

Any comment from me seems superfluous. Adults, even children, know the signs of the seasons. The signs of Our Lord's Second Coming will be evident. All Our Lord is saying is: pay attention to the signs. I'm telling you, in advance, what they will be. *Furthermore,* I'm also telling you that when the signs of my coming are readily discernible by average, ordinary people, and even children, then I can assure you that all the events of which I have spoken will occur within the space of *one* generation. St. Luke, Chapter 21, Verses 28–32, tells us that when THESE THINGS BEGIN TO HAPPEN . . . THE PRESENT GENERATION will not pass away until ALL this takes place.

All I can tell you is that the signs of Our Lord's second advent seem readily discernible now. The storm warnings are up. Since forty years is usually considered the measure of one generation— then, all those latter day events which were foretold by Our Lord will be occurring NOW in these very times in which we are living.

These signs should not frighten us, however. For Our Lord assures us:

"When these things BEGIN to happen, stand erect and hold your heads high, for your deliverance is near at hand" (Lk. 21:28).

We need have no fear. Do we not long to be with Our Lord? I do. So must you. And now the veil will be lifted and we will finally be with Our Lord always. This is a *wonderful,* a *glorious* day to look forward to.

But to return to the Old Testament prophecies to which I alluded. We, of this present generation, are able to understand, to make sense of, many of the prophecies of the Old Testament (and of the New Testament, as we shall see just a bit later). This, in itself, constitutes a sign of the latter days. In the book of the prophet Daniel we find that Daniel is told: "to keep secret the message and seal it until the end time . . . Go, Daniel . . . because the words are to be kept secret and sealed until the end time. Many shall be refined, purified and tested, but the wicked shall prove wicked: NONE OF THEM SHALL HAVE UNDERSTANDING, BUT THE WISE SHALL HAVE IT" (Dan. 12:4–10).

Now, for the first time in history, the prophecies of the Old and New Testament which relate to the latter days are, for the most part, *beginning* to make sense. The book of Daniel is being unsealed—at least for those who are willing to stop, take a look, try to put two and two together.

Of course, if you aren't happy with the prophetic message in Daniel, you can turn to St. Paul who says the same thing:

"You are not in the dark, brothers, that the day (the Day of the Lord) should catch you off guard, like a thief" (1 Thess. 5:4).

Another sign of the latter days will be the rebuilding of the temple. I mention this now, and somewhat in passing, since there does exist some question as to whether or not this will start prior to or after the Rapture of the Church. It is a possibility that the rebuilding of the temple will begin prior to the Rapture and be completed after the Rapture. In any case, Our Lord foretold the destruction of the Temple and of Jerusalem. This utter destruction of the Temple and the city did occur forty years after Our Lord died on the cross. However, when Our Lord spoke of the end-time, one of the things he said was:

"When you see the abomination of desolation, which was spoken of by Daniel the prophet, STANDING IN THE HOLY PLACE (the Temple in Jerusalem)—let him who reads understand—then let those who are in Judea flee to the mountains . . ." (Mt. 24:15–16).

Several assumptions have to be made by us, the readers (even as St. Matthew says: let those who read understand). If the abomination of desolation is going to be standing on holy ground (that is, in the temple) there is going to have to be a temple for him to stand in. Therefore—the rebuilding of the temple.

St. Paul also speaks of "that son of perdition who seats himself in God's temple and even declares himself to be God . . ." (2 Thess. 2:3–4).

Again, if, during the end-time, the son of perdition is going to seat himself in the temple, there is going to have to be a temple in which he is going to seat himself and proclaim himself God. Therefore—the rebuilding of the Temple.

It then follows that if the Temple is going to be rebuilt (and it will be rebuilt, have no fear!) then the Jews, the Jewish nation, will have to be back in the Promised Land and they will also have to have possession of the city of Jerusalem. No comment is needed here. The Nation of Israel was once again re-established in Palestine in 1948. In 1967 Israel regained possession of the city of Jerusalem.

This particular return of *some* of the Jewish people to the land is a return in unbelief. Again, this is simply fulfilling an ancient prophecy. Learned commentators and great, voluminous, scholarly commentaries to the contrary notwithstanding, the inspired word of Scripture indicates, by way of the prophetic vision of Ezekiel (Ezek. 36:16–38) that Israel will be restored to the land. The Lord God scattered the Nation Israel (the Jewish people) among the nations, dispersed them into foreign lands. This happened as a punishment. However, for the sake of His Holy Name, the Lord God promised that He would bring the Jewish people back from among the nations, gather them in from ALL the foreign lands (not Babylon) and place them in their own land.

Therefore, according to the prophecy, there is, first of all, a return to the land by some, and only some, Jewish people, in unbelief, who will prepare the land for the eventual return of *all* the Jewish people, not in unbelief but believing in the Lord God. This second ingathering of all the Jewish people will *begin* after the Russian invasion, three and a half years after the Rapture. But there will be a dreadful persecution and another scattering, another dispersal. *Only then, after all this has happened to them,* will *all* the Jews be brought back to the Holy Land. We will speak of this in far greater detail later on and in proper chronological order. Suffice it to say that it will be at the second ingathering that the Lord God will sprinkle the Jewish people with clean water, cleanse them from their impurities, and give them a new spirit and a new heart.

It is Ezekiel who so prophesies in that famous vision, the vision of the dry bones. Ezekiel saw himself in the center of a plain filled with the bones of the dead (and long since dead since they were so dry). The Lord God told him to prophesy over the bones and say to them: "Dry bones, hear the word of the Lord." The Lord God then caused the bones to come together. (The old gospel song keeps going through my head: ankle bone connected with the shin bone, shin bone connected with the knee bone, knee bone connected with the thigh bone, now hear the word of the Lord. A great song, but very distracting!) In any case, to continue. The Lord God then caused sinews and flesh to come upon those dry bones. Then He covered them with skin. Please note that at this point these nicely reconstructed bodies are without life. There is no spirit in them. These lifeless bodies represent the Nation Israel restored to the land, BUT in unbelief.

The Lord God then told Ezekiel to say to the spirit: "Thus says the Lord God: From the four winds come, O spirit, and breathe into these slain that they may come to life." Ezekiel did as the Lord God commanded and that vast army of people came alive and stood upright. The Nation Israel would now possess the land in belief (in God, not in Our Lord, that is). The Lord God, speaking to the Jewish people through Ezekiel, says:

"O my people, I will open your graves and have you rise from them and bring you back to the land of Israel. Then you shall know that I am the Lord, when I open your graves and have you rise from them, O my people. I will put my spirit in you that you may live, and I will settle you upon your land; thus you know that I am the Lord. I HAVE PROMISED AND I WILL DO IT, SAYS THE LORD" (Ezek. 37:1–14).

Israel shall be returned to the land and shall reclaim it. Indeed, the reclamation of the land is going on in startling manner at this very moment. The prophecy of Amos is being fulfilled:

"I will bring about the restoration of my people, Israel; they shall rebuild and inhabit their ruined cities, plant vineyards and drink the wine, set out gardens and eat the fruits" (Amos 9:14–15).

In the strict sense this is a prophecy which is to be fulfilled in the Millennial kingdom, the thousand year reign of Our Lord upon earth which follows upon His Second Coming. (All of which makes me wonder. Since we are witnessing the beginnings of the fulfillment of a prophecy which very obviously will be completely fulfilled only in the Millennial kingdom, can that Millennial kingdom be far distant? Nevertheless we can see the beginnings of its fulfillment right now.)

In Leviticus we find that the Lord God levels some very dire threats against the nation Israel should the Israelites disobey Him. As we all know from our Bible History, the Israelites did disobey the Lord God and punishments did follow. The cities of the nation were laid waste, the sanctuaries were devastated, the people scattered among the nations. When the people have made proper amends for their guilt, however, the Lord God will remember His covenant with Jacob, His covenant with Isaac, His covenant with Abraham.

"Yet even so, even while they are in their enemies' land, I will not reject or spurn them, lest by wiping them out, I make void my covenant with them; for I, the Lord, am their God" (Lev. 26:44).

This is a guarantee by God that the Jews would never become extinct, or be absorbed into the nations. This has been fulfilled, thus far, for over 2000 years.

No matter how strange it may sound, no matter how adverse the conditions, no matter how contrary to reality it may seem, the Jewish people are to possess the Promised Land by reason of the covenants of the Lord. And, now, of course, they do possess the land again. Somehow, if not this way then that way, the Bible prophecies will be fulfilled. And, from the look of things, to the letter.

But—keep firmly in mind what I have already pointed out. *Some* of the Jewish people are restored to the land. *Some* of the Jewish people will cultivate the land. *Then* the nation Israel will suffer persecution once again, as will all the Jewish people, in the time of the Day of the Lord. Given the thrust of a number of prophecies, Jews will have to be back on the land *and also* priests will have to be offering worship in the Temple, if the details of the prophetic message are valid. Consider, for example, Joel's words:

> Blow the trumpet in Zion!
> proclaim a fast,
> call an assembly;
> Gather the people,
> notify the congregation;
> Assemble the elders,
> gather the children
> and the infants at the breast;
> Let the bridegroom quit his room,
> and the bride her chamber.
> Between the porch and the altar
> let the priests, the ministers of the
>   Lord, weep,
> And say, "Spare, O Lord, your people,
> and make not your heritage a reproach,
> with the nations ruling over them!
> Why should they say among the peoples,
> 'Where is their God?' "
>
> (Joel 2:15–17)

The distressing events of which Joel speaks occur after the Rapture and during the time period known as the Day of the Lord. Why then discuss this text, this problem now, in a chapter about preliminary signs? The text simply assumes the existence of: a nation, a family life, a temple, a priestly class. All these are the elements of a society as it is quite usually, ordinarily structured. To achieve such a functioning society requires a reasonable amount of time. From this it follows quite logically that such a functioning society had its beginnings in the time prior to the Rapture. The time period between the Rapture of the Church and the Russian invasion of Israel (3½ years) could not be described as "a reasonable period of time," especially when you consider the numerous and horrendous events which will be taking place then.

The same line of reasoning applies to yet another prophecy. I know it is just plain common sense and most of you will think it somewhat silly of me to belabor the obvious. But a reader here or there might otherwise miss the point. So please bear with me.

First, let me quote a rather well-known prophecy from Ezekiel about certain events of the latter days (and about which I will have a few more things to say later on in the book).

Then shall those who live in the cities of Israel go out and burn weapons: . . . for SEVEN years they shall make fires with them. THEY SHALL NOT HAVE TO BRING IN WOOD FROM THE FIELDS OR CUT IT DOWN IN THE FORESTS, for they shall make fires with the weapons (Ezek. 39:9–10).

That the inhabitants of Israel will be able to cut down wood in the forests means—there will have to be forests! But until fairly recently Palestine was, by and large, a barren wasteland! Now, however, there are forests. By 1960 some one hundred million (100,000,000!) trees had been planted throughout the land.

(1) The seven-year period mentioned in Ezekiel will begin three and a half years after the Rapture.

(2) I know a Sister of Charity (of Jewish parentage and who teaches in a well-known Catholic University in South Orange, New Jersey), who has a section of a forest in Israel named after her because she donated 100 trees toward the reforesting of the Promised Land.

(3) The question arises, why are the Israelites burning wood, rather than oil? Intriguing, no?

Since some of these trees are by now close to thirty years old, they are a quite respectable size. Therefore the forests of Israel are a quite respectable size. But then they would have to be of a reasonable size *prior* to the Rapture if they will be large enough to be worked for fuel *after* the Rapture, as Ezekiel tells us they will be. Therefore—the reforesting of Israel is a most significant preliminary sign of the latter days.

I think I shall add here Isaiah's prophecy that the desert will bloom as the rose, even though it applies more fittingly to the millennial age:

The wilderness and the parched land will exult; the desert shall rejoice and blossom as the rose. They will bloom with abundant flowers and rejoice with joyful song.

The glory of Lebanon will be given to them, the splendor of Carmel and Sharon; they will see the glory of the Lord, the splendor of our God (Is. 35:1–2).

This also is beginning to take place now, for the first time in thousands of years.

Some of the preliminary signs are not yet completely fulfilled, although we are quite aware that they are beginning to be fulfilled. One preliminary sign, so it would seem, has not yet arisen—even in its infant or beginning stages. But this is to speak of this sign in a formal manner. That sign—the apostasy, the great falling away. It is true that, as of the moment, we do not have a *formal* apostasy, definite Church leaders preaching definite deviations from true Church doctrine. For what it is worth, I think we do have an apostasy taking place, an *informal* apostasy, with no definite leaders and no definitive deviations from established Church dogma. There is, to my mind, just simply a great falling away. No leaders. No dogmas. Just a lot of people not going to church. There does exist, of course, a moral problem. The statistics published in a scientific study of the problem by Greeley, McCready and McCourt (1976) show that there has been a very significant drop in church attendance by Catholic people in the years 1965 through 1974. In 1965, 67% of Catholics attended church at least weekly. By 1974 that figure had declined to 55%. This particular study indicates one of the major reasons for the decline was the publication of the Papal encyclical Humanae Vitae with its highly unpopular ruling on birth control.

In this present day drastic changes have occurred in our society's approach to marriage, divorce, birth control, sexual mores, abortion. I would venture to state that a majority of people (Catholic people, that is) do not look to the Church any longer for guidance on these matters. I think that probably a majority of Catholic people simply ignore the Church's teaching in these moral questions. Many form and follow their own consciences, being influenced far more by the secular society in which they live than by the Church.

(I might add that any Roman Catholic priest could tell you of the startling decline in the use of the confessional over the past few years.)

Another good example is the infiltration of TM (Transcendental Meditation) into the Church. TM is a religious system, with a "world plan," and proposes to its adherents the Guru Dev as a mediator between God and man. In practice and theory, it runs absolutely counter to the tenets of Christianity. Yet this religious system is embraced and taught eagerly in some Catholic schools and colleges and monasteries.

Its Christian adherents claim it helps them to focus on the risen Christ. In reality, TM ignores Christ, bypasses Him. TM's Christian adherents claim that in our classical Christian systems of spirituality too much emphasis is placed on Our Lord's crucifixion and death. But there is no Easter Sunday unless first there is a Good Friday. And what ever happened to St. Paul's statement in 1 Corinthians 1:22–23, "Yes, Jews demand 'signs' and Greeks look for 'wisdom,' but we preach Christ crucified . . ."?

I could go on and on. But why? No one will listen and there I have the perfect example of Apostasy in the modern style.

Given all the evidence (which I have only hinted at here) Father Andrew Greeley, a noted sociologist, has often declared that the Church is, indeed, suffering from a very real apostasy at the present time. My colleague doesn't agree with me. He thinks there will be a formal, visible break. But I think Father Greeley is right.

And I note with no little interest Maritain's reference to the "neo-modernist fever" in his book *The Peasant of the Garonne* a description, not only of certain Protestant intellectuals, but also of certain "advanced Catholic thinkers," who are intent upon remaining Christian at all costs (even though they really aren't). All of which gives us, to use Maritain's phrase, "a kind of *'immanent' apostasy.*" Fascinating!

But this is precisely the kind of apostasy needed if the prophecies of St. John about the apostate church and the anti-Pope are to be fulfilled. It surely seems to fit.

I had better quote, now, St. Paul's own words:

"On the question of the coming of Our Lord Jesus Christ and our being gathered to him, we beg you, brothers, not to be so easily agitated or terrified, whether by an oracular utterance, or rumor, or a letter alleged to be ours, into believing that the day of the Lord is here.

"Let no one seduce you, no matter how. Since the MASS APOSTASY has not yet occurred nor the man of lawlessness been revealed—that son of perdition and adversary who exalts himself

above every so-called god proposed for worship, he who seats himself in God's temple and even declares himself to be God—do you
not remember how I used to tell you about these things when I was
still with you? You know what restrains him until he shall be revealed in his own time. The secret force of lawlessness is already at
work, mind you, but there is one who holds him back until that
restrainer shall be taken from the scene. Thereupon the lawless one
will be revealed, and the Lord Jesus will destroy him with the
breath of his mouth and annihilate him by manifesting his own
presence. This lawless one will appear as part of the workings of
Satan, accompanied by all the power and signs and wonders at the
disposal of falsehood—by every seduction the wicked one can devise for those destined to ruin because they have not opened their
hearts to the truth to be saved. Therefore God is sending upon them
a perverse spirit which leads them to give credence to falsehood, so
that all who have not believed the truth but have delighted in
evildoing will be condemned" (2 Thess. 2:1–12).

So—you can see for yourselves that St. Paul, in this section of his
letter to the members of the early Church who lived in Thessalonica, tells them (and hence, us) not to be disturbed or agitated,
not to be terrified that they have not been gathered to the Lord. The
Day of the Lord has not yet occurred. A number of things are clear.
St. Paul is speaking of the Second Coming of the Lord. At this time
Our Lord will destroy the evil one. St. Paul also is telling us that
prior to the Second Coming the evil one will exercise power, authority on this earth and upon the people alive at that time, upon all
the people not gathered to the Lord. Therefore St. Paul is telling us
that, prior to the role of the evil one during the Day of the Lord,
there will occur that event we call the Rapture, the gathering up of
those who are true Christians to be with the Lord.

Also, please note why St. Paul can reassure the Thessalonians
(and hence, us) that they have not missed the Rapture. The great
apostasy, the great falling-away, has not yet occurred and, too, that
which restrains the man of sin has not yet been taken away.

We have already taken a look at the apostasy problem, the great
falling-away from the Church. The only point I would like to add to
what we have already said is that eventually one-third of all Church
members and one-third of all Bishops will apostasize, fall away,
from true Church doctrine, according to Revelations, Chapter 12,
Verse 4. It will be easy for all this to happen because radical
theologians (some even deliberately) have been working toward
this split, this apostasy, for a good five to ten years now. (There is
one I know who even uses sex as a tool to achieve this end.)

As to the restrainers, we are simply uncertain as to what St. Paul means. Perhaps he is referring to all Church members (the mystical Body of Christ indwelt by the Holy Spirit) in the state of grace who, thereby, thwart the intentions of the evil one. Once these Church members have been raptured all hell will quite literally break loose.

Beyond this, I do not care to conjecture. I only hope and pray that I will be amongst those who are raptured, caught up to meet the Lord. I hope and pray you are too. It is not going to be very pleasant here once the Rapture has occurred.

The next preliminary sign we must study is that which is called the Ten Nation Federation. The Old Testament book of Daniel is essential for an understanding of this sign. So let's turn to Daniel (Dan. 2:31–45) and see what he has to tell us. Daniel had to make known the dream of King Nebuchadnezzar and then he had to interpret it. The Lord God revealed all of this to Daniel. Thus he was able to tell the king that the dream foretold "what will be in the LATTER DAYS." The dream, then, deals with the end-time, the Day of the Lord, the end of the age. As to the dream: the king saw a mighty image of exceeding brightness. It was frightening to behold. The head of this image was of fine gold, the breast and arms were of silver, its belly and thighs of bronze, its legs were of iron and its feet partly of iron and partly of clay. As the king looked on, a stone not hewn out by human hand smote the image on its feet and broke it into pieces. Then all the parts of the image were broken into pieces and scattered so that nothing of the image remained. However, the stone which struck the image became a great mountain and filled the whole earth.

Daniel then interpreted the dream: he told the king that he, the king, was the head of gold. After the king, another kingdom would arise, inferior to his own. Then a third kingdom would arise which would rule over the whole earth. And then there would be a fourth kingdom, a kingdom as strong as iron because iron can shatter and crush all things. The feet and toes, being partly of iron and partly of clay, signified a divided kingdom, partly strong and partly brittle. But as iron does not mix with clay so these divided kingdoms would not hold together. Then the Lord God would set up a kingdom which will never be destroyed. It will bring all the other kingdoms to an end, even as the stone destroyed the image in the king's dream.

Daniel was granted yet another and terrifying vision (Dan. 7:1–8) wherein he saw four immense beasts emerge from the great sea. The first beast was like a lion but it had eagles' wings. The second beast was like a bear. It was raised up on one side and among the teeth in its mouth were three tusks. The third beast was like a leopard except that on its back it had four wings and also it had four heads.

Daniel describes the fourth beast by saying that it was different from all the others, it was terrifying, horrible, and of extraordinary strength. It devoured and crushed with its great iron teeth and what was left it trampled with its feet. This beast had ten horns projecting from its head. As Daniel was looking at these horns, another horn, a little horn, sprang up in the midst of them and three of them were torn away to make room for the little horn.

The two visions deal with the same order of events. The head of gold and the lion represent the Babylonian empire. The arms of silver in the first vision and the bear of the second vision represent the empire of the Medes and the Persians. The trunk of brass and the leopard signify the empire of Greece. Finally the legs of iron and the beast with the iron teeth represent the Roman Empire. Despite the learned commentaries which say otherwise, the ten toes and the ten horns signify the confederation of nations which will be in existence at the time of the anti-Christ and the end-times. These ten confederated nations will stem from the Roman Empire of old. The precise manner, shape, form of the confederation remains uncertain. It is the fact of a ten nation federation which is certain. These ten nations are those lands, those nations, that territory once occupied by the Roman Empire at the peak of its power in classical times. Also these ten nations will be divided, five and five. Five will be in the east, five will be in the west.

The fact of this ten nation alliance, which has never occurred in the past, receives rather strong and quite reasonable confirmation in St. John's book of Revelation. St. John speaks of the beast which will exist again and he points out that the seven heads of the beast of his vision signify the seven hills on which the woman sits enthroned (Rev. 17:9). One city, and one city only, is world famous for its location upon seven hills—Rome.

Rome will be the capital of the anti-Christ, at least for a while. Of course, just to complete the picture a bit, the stone which became a mountain and filled the whole earth, in Daniel, Chapter 2, Verse 35, signifies the kingdom of God which destroys the kingdom of Anti-Christ. But of this more later.

Here again, we are concerned only with preliminary signs. Later developments we will consider later, all in proper chronological sequence.

It would now seem reasonable to point out, as so many commentators do, that in the European Common Market we have at least the *beginnings* of the ten nation confederation.

I might add one further point before turning to the two remaining preliminary signs we have yet to consider. At some point during the ten and a half years between the Rapture and the Second Coming, Russia will attack the Nation Israel. We will discuss this in its proper chronological place. My point in mentioning it here is that if Russia is going to attack and invade Israel shortly *after* the Rapture *then* Russia has to be in a favorable position to do that *before* the Rapture. And, as we are all well aware, for the first time in history Russia is in a favorable position to attack Israel, should she wish to do so. This has never been the case before. Only since World War II has she had the mobility, only since 1948 has there been an Israel to attack. Interesting, no? Yes, very!

We turn now to a consideration of Anti-Christ. Anti-Christ—the Abomination of Desolation—will show his *true* colors only after the Rapture and the time when that which restrains is taken away. Here, too, a certain natural course of events, a certain natural development has to be allowed for, a rather natural growth. Therefore, Anti-Christ will be a known, perhaps well-known, leader on the world scene prior to the Rapture. We must consider Anti-Christ, then, under preliminary signs. It is our view that Anti-Christ is now here, one who is preparing for the role of a great world leader, a masterful politician, a prince for the people and one who will emerge on the world scene to obtain for nations and peoples world peace and personal security.

In Daniel (Chapter 8, Verses 23–25), we are told that in the appointed time of the end a leader shall arise who will be of bold countenance, who will understand and be able to solve that which would seem unsolvable. He will have great power, he will cause fearful destruction and he will be successful in what he does. He will destroy mighty men and even the people of the saints. He will be deceitful and cunning. He will magnify himself. Without giving any warning he will destroy many and, finally, he will rise up against the Prince of princes. However, in the end, he will be broken, but by no human hand.

There we have a frightening description of a great and forceful leader who is, in reality, a satanic tyrant. Notice that he is wily, crafty; he will artfully lead many astray, drawing them to himself by his cunning, his deviousness. Then—when he has achieved power and authority, he will destroy others—other world leaders—and

also—notice—the people of the saints. He will, therefore, be a persecutor of the Jews, since the word "saints" in the Old Testament
always means the Jews.

This is the same leader who is symbolized earlier in Daniel by
the little horn of Daniel's vision. We have already looked at that
passage and I simply want to remind you that this little horn took
the place of—that is, destroyed—three of the ten original horns of
the beast of Daniel's vision. So, Anti-Christ will destroy mighty
men who oppose him. Anti-Christ will war with the saints and will
prevail over them until the Second Coming. The loyal members of
the *True* Church—those who remain on earth following the
Rapture—will be most severely and cruelly persecuted for their
faith. Many will suffer martyrdom for Our Lord (Rev. 6:9).

The martyr's crown is a glorious one, I know. I hope—should I be
found wanting and I am not caught up with the saints to meet Our
Lord at the moment of the Rapture—that I will have the strength
and the faith to persevere and, finally, save my soul. I pray that you,
too, will persevere and save your immortal soul. All things considered, however, I do pray to the Lord that I will be prepared at
the moment of the Rapture of the Church. Be prepared! You do not
know the day or the hour!

In the passage from St. Paul's second letter to the Thessalonians,
which we have taken a quick look at, St. Paul speaks of the lawless
one, the son of perdition. There St. Paul tells us that all those who
refuse to love the truth will perish. They will not be saved. We can
be saved only by standing firm and holding fast to the traditions
given to us by St. Paul through God's own Church, through our
sanctification by the Spirit, and belief in the truth.

St. John, speaking of the persecution of the saints by Anti-Christ,
says, "Here is a call for the endurance and faith of the saints" (Rev.
12:10).

Now we turn to the last of the preliminary signs. Here I want to
quote St. Paul:

"But as to the times and the seasons, brethren, you have no need
to have anything written to you. For you yourselves know well that
the day of the Lord will come like a thief in the night. WHEN
PEOPLE SAY, 'THERE IS PEACE AND SECURITY,' then sudden destruction will come upon them as travail comes upon a woman with
child, and there will be no escape. BUT YOU ARE NOT IN DARKNESS,
BRETHREN, FOR THAT DAY TO SURPRISE YOU LIKE A THIEF. For you
are all sons of light; we are not of the night or of darkness" (1 Thess.
5:1–5). RSV

The additional clue, the extra preliminary sign we glean from this text is that of "peace and security." St. Paul warns us that just at the moment when we are ready to sit back and rest on our laurels, just when we finally achieve some sense of security for ourselves and the world in which we live, just when we achieve a certain peace for ourselves and the world in which we live, just as we are relaxing, enjoying our good fortune, our material possessions, just as we are patting ourselves on the back and telling ourselves that we need no longer fear war or the insecurities of troubled times—THEN! SUDDENLY!!

The Day of the Lord will come as the thief in the night.

As recorded in St. Matthew, Our Lord said much the same thing. He said that when the Son of Man comes it will be as it was in the days of Noah. In those days, prior to the flood, people were going about focusing their attention on worldly concerns. They were eating and drinking, marrying and giving in marriage up until the very day when Noah entered the ark. They had little or no concern for God's affairs and the voice of prophecy. It is the same now (Mt. 24:36-40).

St. Luke adds a further detail. At the time of the Day of the Lord, the coming of the Son of Man, it will be as it was in the days of Lot. People were eating and drinking, buying and selling, planting and building. Then—suddenly, the destructive fire and sulfur (Lk. 17:28). It is of interest to note that St. Luke, in his description of the days of Lot, does *not* mention marrying and the giving in marriage. For varied reasons the description is quite apropos for our present society. Consider these texts:

"And look at the guilt of your sister Sodom: she and her daughters were proud, sated with food, complacent in their prosperity, and they gave no help to the poor and needy. Rather, they became haughty and committed abominable crimes in my presence; then as you have seen, I removed them" (Ezek. 16, 49-50).

Genesis, Chapter 18, Verse 20, speaks of the gravity of the sin of Sodom.

Genesis 6:1-3 and Genesis 6:12-13 point to the violence, the sexual disorders and general corruption prevalent on the earth prior to the days of Noah. And the latter days will be as the time of Noah and of Lot. In the latter days, too, Isaiah points out that "their sin like Sodom they vaunt, they hide it not" (Is. 3:9). (Certainly in these our days the Gay Liberation Movement is very active, its members parading about, vaunting their sexual activities. You may draw your own conclusions!)

In 2 Timothy 3:1-7, we read:

"Do not forget this: there will be terrible times in the last days.

Men will be lovers of self and of money, proud, arrogant, abusive, disobedient to their parents, ungrateful, profane, inhuman, implacable, slanderous, licentious, brutal, hating the good. They will be treacherous, reckless, pompous, lovers of pleasure rather than of God as they make a pretense of religion but negate its power."

All the preliminary signs are present save the last, the sign of peace and security. This we do not have. From the looks of things it may be a while before we achieve some semblance of peace and security. Of course we are now at peace here in the United States. We have security, I guess. But there is no peace and security in many places around the world, and especially in the Middle East. I would think that we will not have this final sign present in the world until there is peace and security in the Middle East, at the very least. And it could well be that Anti-Christ himself will help to achieve the very peace and security which should alert us to the fact that the Rapture is at hand. But then so should the 4th sign, the Apostasy.

Thus, we may achieve peace and security in the Middle East quite suddenly and sooner than we think. Who am I to say? or you either?

In any case, it would seem that all the signs preliminary to the Rapture and the Second Coming of Our Lord are present, save one. That final sign could be present at any time. The wise man or woman will, therefore, heed the words of St. Mark:

> Watch therefore—for you do not know when the master of the house will come, in the evening, or at midnight, or at cockcrow, or in the morning— lest he come suddenly and find you asleep. AND WHAT I SAY TO YOU I SAY TO ALL: WATCH (Mk. 13:35–36). RSV

ALL—I repeat—ALL the preliminary signs must be in place and operative before you can make the statement that the Rapture is truly at hand and the Second Coming imminent. If even one sign is not present and operative then you have to wait until it is present and operative.

ALL these must be present:

(1) False Christs, wars, rumors of war, commotions, famine, plague, earthquakes.
(2) The destruction of the Temple, the need for a new Temple.
(3) The return of *some* of the Jewish people to the Promised Land.
(4) The apostasy.
(5) The ten nation federation.

(6) The emergence of the great world leader (Anti-Christ); keep in mind he will not be recognized for what he is until after the Rapture.

(7) The time of peace and security; this for a brief time *following* upon the first signs, wars and rumors of war; Anti-Christ will bring about this time of peace and security.

If ALL these signs are present on the world scene and if ALL these are operative signs—that is, if these are active signs, actually occurring, going on—THEN AND ONLY THEN can you say that the moment has arrived, the BIRTH is at hand. The signs are like the BIRTH PANGS, at first irregular and far apart, then more regularly and more and more frequently. Remember, all these things are not yet clear. The beginnings of the 4th and 5th signs seem to be present now. When all this gels, when all these signs do fall into place, events can move very quickly.

While one or the other, or several of these signs have occurred in the past, they have never all occurred together. Certainly the Jews were not in Israel. If things do not gel soon, one or the other of these signs will soon disappear again, and it will be a long time before they re-occur simultaneously again. It does not seem likely that all these signs will reappear continually in the future; then they would not be a diagnostic sign of the times, something we are to look for.

Those are the clues. The rest is up to you. With Our Lord all we can say is: Be Prepared! Watch!! (Mk. 13:32)

IV

Raptured!

We have spoken of the RAPTURE OF THE CHURCH so frequently in previous chapters that you must be tired of hearing the phrase. Yet this is THE moment in our lives, if we are alive at this time. The purpose of the Rapture is to lead us away from the dangers that could befall us should we have to endure the terrible trials that will envelop mankind at this time. To those in the state of mortal sin, it should serve as a warning to rectify their lives. If we are in the state of sanctifying grace, we will be caught up to meet Our Lord and to be with Him always. If we are not in the state of grace, if we have mortal sin on our souls, then we will miss the Rapture and then— we will have to endure the ten and one-half years of persecution and tribulation. These we will have to withstand if we expect to be able to meet and be with Our Lord at the actual moment of His Second Coming.

We know, of course, that these events—the Rapture and the Second Coming—are two separate occurrences. We are told by St. John, in his book of Revelation: "Behold, he is coming with the clouds, and every eye will see him, everyone who pierced him, and all tribes of the earth will wail on account of him" (Rev. 1:7).

Here we have an account of the Second Coming. In the first place this event will be seen by *all* the peoples of the earth who are yet alive. Furthermore when these people do see Our Lord coming they will be terrified and will cry out in terror.

We can also know of the actual time of the Second Coming with reasonable accuracy, making a common sense judgment and basing this judgment upon the events which precede the moment of that Second Coming. (It is these events which we will discuss in the chapters to follow.) Yet St. Paul tells us, indeed, Our Lord tells us, that we do not know the day or the hour. The Day of the Lord will come as a thief in the night (1 Thess. 5:2).

I'm sure that it is at once obvious to you that two different events are being described. Otherwise we would have contradictory evidence about one event from the inspired pages of the Scriptures. To come on the clouds of heaven in the sight of all the peoples of the world is not exactly the same thing as to come as a thief in the night. No, not exactly.

To stand in terror at the sight of the Second Coming of Our Lord does not have exactly the same kind of meaning as St. Luke's injunction: "Arise, lift up your heads! Your redemption is at hand" (Lk. 21:28). The one sentence denotes fear, the other joy. These are two very different emotions—at least to my way of thinking. No, there is simply no question about it. In a number of the passages of Scripture (about the Second Coming) we have to understand that we are being given details of two events, albeit the details are given by way of prophetic vision.

I note, therefore, again, the difficulty of reading and grasping that which is discussed in terms of, by means of, such prophetic vision. The prophet is looking at events far in the future. He can see and relate for us the two events. However he sees these events as occurring at one and the same time, as it were. Intervals of time and space collapse and two events widely separated by space and time can appear as elements of what is seemingly one event. In reality, two or even more events are being described. It is like looking through the wrong end of a telescope. All perspective disappears.

The second letter of St. Peter contains a good example of this problem of reading aright that which is reported through prophetic vision. St. Peter speaks of the Day of the Lord which will come like a thief. Then he adds that the heavens will pass away with a loud noise and the elements will be dissolved with fire. Then he goes on to tell us to do all that we can to hasten the Day of the Lord—when everything is to be enkindled and dissolved with fire! (2 Pt. 3:11–13).

Not able to determine the time periods involved, St. Peter is, nevertheless, aware that two different things have to be going on. It just doesn't make good sense to hasten the day when one is going to get burned up, dissolved with fire. Simple comparisons with other New Testament texts confirm the opinion that St. Peter is, indeed, telling of two events, the Day of the Lord—the Rapture, that is—and the events which occur at the end of the millennium—the thousand-year reign of Our Lord, that is.

The Rapture, then, is related to the Second Coming and also the millennial kingdom. However, it is a separate event. Among the numerous texts which allude to the Rapture in one way or another,

St. Paul's first letter to the Thessalonians contains, perhaps, the clearest reference to it. I had best quote that text in full:

"We would have you clear about those who sleep in death, brothers; otherwise you might yield to grief, like those who have no hope. For if we believe that Jesus died and rose, God will bring forth with him from the dead those also who have fallen asleep believing in him. We say to you, as if the Lord himself had said it, THAT WE WHO LIVE, WHO SURVIVE UNTIL HIS COMING, will in no way have an advantage over those who have fallen asleep. No, the Lord himself will come down from heaven at the word of command, at the sound of the archangel's voice and God's trumpet; and those who have died in Christ will rise first. Then we the living, THE SURVIVORS, WILL BE CAUGHT UP WITH THEM in the clouds to meet the Lord in the air. Thenceforth we shall be with the Lord unceasingly" (1 Thess. 4:13–17).

I will now give you that quotation in Latin. You will see immediately why the moment of being caught up to meet the Lord is called the Rapture. It is derived from the Latin word for "we shall be caught up," *rapiemur*. "Rapture" is the English noun derived from the Latin verb "rapiemur," which is closely related to the Greek word "Harpasdo." This word, used here by St. Paul, is used by St. John in Revelation 12, Verse 5, of the Rapture of the "maleson." (Of this we will speak later.) But you can see this for yourselves. Here is the final sentence of the quotation in Latin:

"Deinde nos, qui vivimus, qui relinquimur SIMUL RAPIEMUR cum illis in nubibus obviam Christo in aera, et sic semper cum Domino erimus" (1 Thess. 4:17).

The passage needs little commentary. St. Paul is telling the Thessalonians that if they live as they should they will be *caught up* to meet Our Lord. The dead will rise. Those who are alive at Our Lord's coming will also be caught up to be with Our Lord. Please note the phrasing. St. Paul does *not say* that those who are alive at this moment will first die, be brought back to life, *then* caught up to meet with Our Lord. He *does* say that those who are dead will be brought back to life. *Then* those of us who are alive will also be caught up—*without having died!*

St. Paul adds the fact that the Day of the Lord comes like the thief. We cannot know the day or the hour. *However*—we can be prepared. We are not in the dark. We are children of light (1 Thess. 5:1–7). We are also supposed to read the signs of the times.

We have already looked at the statements of St. Paul in his second letter to the Thessalonians. As you recall, in this letter St. Paul reassures the people of Thessalonica that they have not been bypassed, overlooked by Our Lord. The Day of the Lord has not yet occurred. The Thessalonians apparently had been led to believe that the Day of the Lord had arrived. Yet here they were—still working, struggling, living upon this earth and, as St. Paul says, they were terrified. Why terrified? Since the members of the early Church believed with a deep and firm conviction in the Parousia— the Second Coming—they were terrified, I should think that they would have to endure the satanic attacks of the lawless one until such time as the lawless one was destroyed by Our Lord.

Remember—a persecution had just started. These recent converts thought this must be anti-Christ's persecution, not realizing there would be a number of persecutions before Anti-Christ should arrive on the scene. It is interesting to note that they were not surprised that St. Paul had been left behind! They knew he was baptized, they knew of his faith; but was he in the state of grace!? A fascinating little footnote in Bible history.

St. Paul spoke in tongues (1 Cor. 14:18), worked miracles (Acts 19:11), preached the faith (2 Cor. 11:7), had visions (2 Cor. 12:2), expelled demons (Acts 16:18). None of these things could guarantee that St. Paul was in the state of grace. Paul was baptized, was a Hebrew, was an Apostle, a bishop, had been persecuted, suffered hardship, preached the gospel for free, no one doubted his faith— yet all this could not ensure that he would be raptured.

Obviously the sure way to be prepared for the Rapture is to be in the state of grace which comes from prayer and the sacraments, obeying the commandments—in a word, practicing virtue and avoiding sin. (Of course St. Paul was really prepared for the Rapture, should it have occurred in his day. He just didn't bother to enlighten the Thessalonians on that point.)

It is reasonably clear that the Thessalonians should have remembered that St. Paul had already given them some clues as to the first in the whole series of events leading up to the Second Coming. St. Paul reminds them that he had preached about the mass apostasy which had yet to occur and also of the first signs of the son of perdition. He also reminds the Thessalonians that they know what is restraining that son of perdition, that once that which restrains him HAS BEEN TAKEN FROM THE SCENE satanic forces will be unleashed upon the world in full diabolical fury (2 Thess. 2:1–12).

As you realize quite well, I'm sure, we do not rely simply on one or two texts from St. Paul. To corroborate St. Paul's thinking we can turn to St. Matthew, as well as to St. Mark, St. Luke, and also to St. John's gospel. When the Evangelists relate Our Lord's description of the end-times, they speak too of the Rapture.

First, let's take a look at Our Lord's words as recorded by St. Luke:

"ON THAT DAY, let him who is on the housetop, with his goods in the house, not come down to take them away; and likewise let him who is in the field not turn back. Remember Lot's wife. Whoever seeks to gain his life will lose it, but whoever loses his life will preserve it. I tell you, IN THAT NIGHT [1] there will be two men in one bed; one will be taken and the other left. There will be two women grinding together; one will be taken and the other left! And they (the disciples) said to him, 'Where, Lord?' He said to them, 'Where the body is, there the eagles will be gathered together' " (Lk. 17:31–37). RSV

This passage finally makes sense when it is pointed out that it refers to the Rapture, not the Second Coming. At the actual event of the Second Coming ALL will be judged. *No one* will be able to flee. What, then, is Our Lord's meaning when He says that one will be taken, the other left. He cannot be referring to the Second Coming when He uses those words. He is saying that one person will be left here upon earth, another person will be TAKEN. And to be taken means one's life is saved—given the entire context of the passage. At His Second Coming it is the good (those converted to Our Lord) who will remain; the evil (those who have rejected Our Lord) will be slain.

Suddenly, too, the use of the word "eagle" makes sense. (All modern translations to the contrary notwithstanding, the Greek word *aetios* means eagle, not vulture—and is translated "eagle" in the Revised Standard Version of the Bible, I might add.) The eagles—those who are *taken*, those who are *caught* up—soar upwards, upwards, as only eagles can, to where the body is—that is, THE BODY OF THE SLAIN LAMB!

Now it makes sense! Of course! The Rapture!

Let's take another look at St. Matthew's 24th Chapter. I know I am being repetitious, but this is most important and cannot be helped.

As you already know—because you've already read about it in this book—ALL the tribes of earth will witness the Second Coming. Yet the Son of Man will come as a thief in the night. As I say, you know the answer to that apparent contradiction because we've already discussed the problem.

St. Matthew then adds:

"Then two men will be in the field; one is taken and the other

---

[1] A hint, perhaps, as to the actual moment of the Rapture—Jerusalem time.

left. Two women will be grinding at the mill; one is taken and one
is left. Watch, therefore, for you do not know on what day Your Lord
is coming" (Mt. 24:40–42).

At this point you no longer need any explanatory words from me.
You yourselves know that this can refer only to the moment of the
Rapture and the beginning of the momentous events which lead to
the Second Coming. Too, we have here a hint, at least, as to the
percentage of the Church which will be raptured, that is, possibly
about half (50%).

Granted the fact of the Rapture, several of Our Lord's parables
now make very good sense indeed. Having related His description
of the latter days and of the Rapture of the Church, the authors of
the synoptic gospels give us—of set purpose, I am very sure—four
parables of Our Lord which describe with some vividness
fictionalized scenes which could well occur in reality at the moment of the Rapture.

In the story of the wicked servant (Mt. 24:45–51) the moral is at
once apparent. The servant had been given charge of the household
while his master was away. The servant saw that his master was
slow in returning and made the decision that his master was delayed. Then he beat his fellow servants; he sat down to eat and
drink with the drunkards. Then the master did return at a time
when the servant was not expecting him. The master then cast out
that wicked servant and put him with the hypocrites where men
will weep and gnash their teeth.

The moral is, of course: Be prepared. Fulfill your duties faith-
fully. You cannot know the day or the hour. The master (Our Lord)
will return suddenly (the moment of the Rapture). Should you be
found wanting you will be left behind with the hypocrites. Then,
indeed, you will weep and moan and decry your fate.

The parable of the ten virgins (Mt. 25:1–12) portrays, with
graphic imagery, the same moral. These ten maidens took their
lamps and went to meet the bridegroom. Five of the maidens were
wise, five foolish. The wise virgins took oil along with them to light
their lamps; the five foolish virgins neglected to do this. As it
turned out, the bridegroom was delayed so they all fell asleep.
Then at midnight the maidens were aroused by the cry that the
bridegroom was now arriving and that they were to come out and
meet him. The wise virgins had oil with which to trim their lamps,
the foolish virgins had none. The wise virgins then advised the
foolish virgins to hurry to the dealers and supply themselves with
the necessary oil. This the foolish virgins did. When they returned
from the dealers they found that those who had been prepared had

already gone into the marriage feast with the bridegroom and now the door was locked. The foolish virgins cried aloud and asked the Lord to let them in. The Lord, however, replied that he did not know them, so they could not enter.

Here, once again, I feel that little commentary is needed. The parable clearly deals with the time of the Rapture, something that is as clear to you, I'm sure, as it is to me. The overriding moral is, of course: Watch, for you do not know the day or the hour. What can I tell you. You can see as well as I that five persons were gathered up to be with the Lord, five were left behind. *All* the virgins (who were, by the way, good people, all of them) knew of the Lord's coming, all were expecting Him, yet none knew precisely when He would arrive. So these virgins all believed, all had faith in the Lord. All had performed the good work of coming to meet the Lord, each one bearing her lamp. So all the virgins would seem to be about the same, save for one difference. That difference, of course, was the fact that five lacked oil with which to light their lamps. Now light is symbolic of Sanctifying Grace. And there, I believe, we have the difference. Five of the virgins were in the state of Sanctifying Grace, five were not. The lesson is an obvious one. After all, we are the light of the world (Mt. 5:14). We can't let our lights go out like the foolish virgins. Sanctifying Grace must be burning brightly in our souls if we are to be prepared to meet Our Lord at the moment of the Rapture and for the marriage feast of the Lamb (Rev. 19:7–9). If you are not familiar with that concept, a perusal of our book *The Glory of His Love* [1] would prove helpful.

I think all of us must be quite familiar with the parables of the talents (Mt. 25:14–30). As you know, in this story the master has gone away having first given one servant five talents, another two talents, and a third one talent. The servants entrusted with the five talents earned another five, the servant given the two talents earned another two. The third servant, however, buried the one talent he had been given in the ground and so was unable to make any return on that which had been given to him. The master, upon returning, was very pleased with the first and second servants. He was very angry with the third servant. Although the servant was able to return the original investment of one talent, the master was not at all pleased. He had expected some return on his investment. This he did not receive. Therefore he cast that servant into the outer darkness.

[1] Tombler and Funk, *The Glory of His Love*, Dimension Books, Denville, N.J., 1973.

At this point I feel sure you can supply your own commentary, probably better than mine, at that. I truly feel that any explanatory comments of mine are almost an embarrassment. Every single one of us has received some gift, some thing, from Our Lord. I do not know what your gift is. It can be anything: being a father, a mother; a carpenter, plumber, a cook; a teacher, an engineer. Even a doctor or a nurse. Maybe even being a priest or a Brother or a Sister. Whatever the gift, each of us has received something. Be we young or old, well or sick, rich or poor, each has a gift—each of us has been given SOMETHING. On that SOMETHING Our Lord expects a return. By our good works we adorn ourselves and give honor to the Giver of the Gift. To be gathered up and given charge of yet greater gifts we *must make* a return on Our Lord's original investment in us. Our good works are our return on that investment. Otherwise, you know, we will be cast into the outer darkness where there is wailing and the gnashing of teeth.

The password is: *Watch.* Our Lord, in a brief little parable likens the moment of the Rapture and the preparation for it to the servants and the doorkeeper charged with the care of the household until the master should return. His command to the porter, that is, the doorkeeper, is: Watch. The time of his coming could be in the evening, or at midnight, or at cockcrow, or in the morning. He will come suddenly. Be alert, be prepared. WATCH (Mk. 13:32–37).

These four parables highlight similar themes and also several different themes about the Rapture. They present, in living color, the SUDDENNESS of the Rapture, the IMPORTANCE of faith AND good works, the NECESSITY of being in the state of Sanctifying Grace. Moreover, they teach with persistent clarity: WATCH! THE LORD IS COMING!!

And do we know what will happen to us when we are caught up to meet Our Lord in the air? We do know—at least in a general sort of way—what will happen to us. After all, we are sealed with the Holy Spirit and await the day of redemption, that day, as St. Paul tells us (Ephesians 4, Verses 17–32). We are to avoid evil and we are to do good lest we sadden the Holy Spirit. We are to do good, to practice virtue, to give good example "as we await our blessed hope, the appearing of the glory of the great God and of Our Savior Christ Jesus" (Tit. 2:13). Our faith, our hope, our baptism, our good works prepare us for the great moment of the Rapture. (Of course, it is we who are adults who have need of those good works [1] St. Paul

---

[1] See also James, Chapter 2, Verses 14–26, on faith and good works. "Be assured, then, that faith without works is as dead as a body without breath."

so frequently mentions. Little baptized children get in for free.) In his first letter to the Corinthians, St. Paul tells us:

"Lo! I tell you a mystery. We SHALL NOT ALL SLEEP (i.e., die), but we SHALL ALL BE CHANGED, in a moment, in the twinkling of an eye, at the last trumpet. For the trumpet will sound, and the dead will be raised imperishable, and we shall be changed. For this perishable nature must put on the imperishable and this mortal nature must put on immortality" (1 Cor. 15:51–53). RSV

Several points in this passage bear further investigation. First, St. Paul introduces the entire passage with the words, "I tell you a mystery." He is going to tell us, then, of something that has been hidden or unknown. St. Paul will reveal to us that which has been kept hidden from the penetrating light of knowledge and understanding. Thus far, good. However, what St. Paul reveals retains an element of the mysterious. We are granted new knowledge, true. Our understanding of this new knowledge remains somewhat shrouded, somewhat hidden, obscured by a mist, as it were. We cannot grasp what he is telling us with full and clear understanding.

St. Paul says that we shall not die! This is startlingly enough. Surely all men must die. But no. St. Paul says otherwise. At the time of the Rapture (and this passage does refer distinctly to the Rapture), the dead will be raised and changed. Then the living (who will not undergo death) will be changed. This is clear knowledge, but to grasp this with our understanding is something that boggles the power of our minds. One very much neglected biblical dogma aids our comprehension, the Rapture of the Church.

Yet another point. We will be changed. What does this mean? We know that we will exchange the perishable for the imperishable, the mortal for the immortal. We will, in a split second of time, be glorified, our bodies will become glorified bodies (i.e., similar to Our Lord's resurrected body), our bodies will be redeemed.

We have already been redeemed, you object. We have been redeemed by Our Lord's death on the cross. Right you are. But you must understand that there are three phases to our redemption: the redemption of our souls, the redemption of our bodies, the redemption of all nature. Our souls were certainly redeemed by Our Lord's death. But St. Paul himself says, in his letter to the Romans, "however, all creation awaits its redemption, and not only all creation, but we ourselves groan inwardly as we await the redemption of our bodies" (Rom. 8:23). So there is a bit more to our redemption than the redemption of our souls. At the moment of the Rapture we are told: Lift up your heads for your redemption is at hand. Our bodies, that is, are about to be redeemed.

The final redemption of all nature will be achieved only at the end of Our Lord's thousand-year reign. It's all in St. Paul if you want to go digging into St. Paul's epistles on your own. (You might try Luke 21:28; Ephesians 4:30; 1 Corinthians 15:50; Revelations 21 and 22 for starters.) And it would be fun to go digging with you. However, this would take us too far afield. Back to the subject at hand.

St. Paul has been speaking of the Rapture and, quite rightly, he adds these famous lines:

> "Death is swallowed up in victory.
> O death, where is thy victory?
> O death, where is thy sting?"
> (1 Cor. 15:54–55)

Though less clear than the New Testament references, especially as set forth by St. Paul, the Rapture is surely alluded to by several of the Old Testament prophets. One passage from the prophet Daniel is reasonably clear. Daniel states that at the time when Michael the great prince shall arise there shall be great troubles such as had never happened before. However everyone whose name is found written in the book will be delivered from these same troubles. Daniel mentions further that the dead shall be raised from the dust, some to everlasting life, some to shame and contempt (Dan. 12:1–2).

Daniel speaks of the latter days throughout most of his prophetic book. Here he is definitely speaking of the latter days since he uses the phrase: at that time. He mentions the fact that this will be a time of trial and tribulation. Every affliction possible will befall the nations as a whole. However—and this is the point of interest at the moment—those whose names are written in the book of life (those in the state of Sanctifying Grace which is the divine self-communication, God's gift of Himself, the Indwelling of the Holy Spirit) will be spared the time of tribulation. Those whose names are not written in the book of life, those not in the state of Sanctifying Grace, will suffer the afflictions of the troubles, the Tribulation.

But this is just what we have been talking about, the Rapture of the Church. As you realize, you would not use the text from Daniel as a definitive proof for the Rapture, but you surely can use it to corroborate the definitive Scripture texts we have already discussed.

In the various books I have read on the subject of the latter days, some of which I have brought to your attention, I have never seen the concept I am about to suggest to you now.

St. John's book of Revelations has the following passage:

"And a great portent appeared in heaven, a woman clothed with the sun, with the moon under her feet, and on her head a crown of twelve stars; she was with child and she cried out in her pangs of birth, in anguish for delivery. And another portent appeared in heaven; behold, a great red dragon, with seven heads and ten horns, and seven diadems upon his heads. His tail swept down a third of the stars of heaven, and cast them to the earth. And the dragon stood before the woman who was about to bear a child, that he might devour her child when she brought it forth; she brought forth a male child, one who is to rule all the nations with a rod of iron, but her child was *caught up* to God and to his throne, and the woman fled into the wilderness, where she has a place prepared by God, in which to be nourished for one thousand two hundred and sixty days" (Rev. 12:1–6). RSV

Now—in this passage we are working with symbols, some of whose meanings we have not yet considered. The woman clothed with the sun is the symbol for the Church. The dragon, of course, is the symbol for Satan. The stars of heaven are symbols for the bishops of the Church, even as the crown of twelve stars upon the woman's head represents the twelve Apostles. Actually these particular symbols are not new; they are fairly commonplace and St. John seems to use them in a rather standard and uniform manner.

What, however, is the meaning of the symbol: the woman gave birth to a "male son"? Yes. That is what the Greek text says: a male son. The Greek also uses a rather unusual grammatical construction at this point. Of the "male son," the Greek text says: "one who was to have ruled with a rod of iron."

A number of commentators say that the male child is Our Lord, but that doesn't make very good sense. The Church did *not* bring forth Our Lord; it was Our Lord Who brought forth the Church. Furthermore, Our Lord is already with God His Father and sits at His right hand. How, then, can He be caught up in the future to be with God when He is with God already. No, to interpret the "male son" as Our Lord doesn't make good sense.

To continue, this "male son" was to have ruled with a rod of iron. Now—the Church has brought forth this "male son" who was to have ruled. Who rules in the Church? The Pope rules in the Church. It is the Pope who is the "male son."

This does seem a likely enough hypothesis. The argument goes as follows: The Church is experiencing a time of troubles and tribulations. One-third of all the bishops have fallen away from the Church, a part of the apostasy we have already discussed. Since

they are Church leaders, we can safely assume that they will cause
many of their followers, religious and laity, to fall away from the
Church also. *Then* the Church experiences a most difficult papal
election (a papal election shortly after an apostasy). However, once
a Pope is elected, the Church, at that time, within that time frame,
is raptured.

The newly elected Pope *was to have ruled.* He never does! He is
caught up to God and His throne. He is raptured!

Of course, all those in the state of Sanctifying Grace are raptured
too. If you or I were raptured this very minute, it would not create
much of a stir. You might like to think that it would, but it wouldn't.
But! A newly elected Pope! And about half the Church with him!
This would really be a great *sign,* and a clear-cut *warning* to those
left behind. A different story, indeed!

Such an occurrence would really be a worldwide warning for the
rest of mankind, and surely for Catholic people, at least. As we have
mentioned previously, the Rapture will serve, among other things,
as a warning to those not fortunate enough to be raptured. This sign
should tell them that, if they are to save their souls now, they must
endure, endure. They must make sure they are properly prepared
for the moment of the Second Coming. They (perhaps you or I!)
have been given fair warning! That Second Coming will be our
final chance!

I have a final thought concerning the Rapture before we turn to a
consideration of the persecutions which will follow the Rapture. St.
John at the beginning of the 14th chapter of his gospel says:

"Do not let your hearts be troubled. Have faith in God and faith
in me. In my Father's house there are many dwelling places;
otherwise, how could I have told you that I was going to prepare a
place for you? I am indeed going to prepare a place for you, and
then I shall come back to take you with me, that where I am you
also may be" (Jn. 14:1–3).

Rejoice! Rejoice! Our Lord has gone to make a place for US—for
YOU, for ME—in His kingdom. My heart leaps upwards with the
sheer joy, the delight of it! I want to laugh and sing and cry and
shout: My Lord has gone to prepare a place for ME! The wild aban-
don of it! To be with Our Lord always. The heart's desire, the soul's
ecstatic longing.

O Lord my God, You only Whom I love and desire!

Yes, Our Lord has gone into His kingdom where there are *many*
mansions, a place for the likes of me—and you, too. For I am little
deserving of a mansion in heaven. Indeed, I have no right to such a
place at all. Yet, I have told Our Lord that I regret my sins, I mourn

the injury I have inflicted. I despise the evil one and spit upon him.

O Lord, You alone do I long to embrace. And that will be possible when You return to take me with You. O Lord, I long for Your return. Come quickly, O Lord Jesus, and take me to Yourself and into Your kingdom where You have prepared a place for me and we can be together forever and ever.

I know You are within me now but I long for that rapturous moment when You return and take me up—and not only me, but all those who love You—to meet You and see You face to face in the air and thus to be with You always.

What an inestimable privilege. Has any other king ever acted in such a manner? Does a lord go ahead of his servant to prepare a place for that servant? Of course not. The servant must go to prepare a place for his lord; then once the lord is settled in and taken care of the servant must fend for himself. Our Lord—as is His wont—has turned things topsy-turvy. HE has gone ahead. Not only has He invited us into His kingdom and, indeed, into His very home, He Himself has prepared that home and made it ready for us. Yet Our Lord did say: "I do not call you servants—but friends!" (Jn. 15:15). Such a thing is almost beyond belief! And at the moment of the Rapture—if we are in the state of Sanctifying Grace—that is precisely what is going to happen to us.

We will enter into our heavenly mansion and we shall be together forever with Our Lord.

O Lord Jesus! Come quickly!

V

Anti-Christ; Anti-Pope

Now we must concern ourselves with the events of the ten and one-half years (approximately) remaining until Our Lord's return, His Second Coming. The Rapture has occurred. Hopefully we ourselves have been gathered up to be with Our Lord.

I must bring your attention to one small problem, however. Even as we do not know the day or the hour of the Rapture, so also, we *cannot* be certain as to the spiritual state of our souls. We can know, more or less, whether or not we have committed serious sin, whether or not we have tried to correct this problem. We can know, more or less, that we have no *serious* sin on our souls, we feel that we have a reasonably close and friendly relationship with Our Lord, with God. Yet, as the Scriptures tell us, we all know sin and imperfection every day of our lives (Jas. 3:2). We fail in so many small ways so many times a day. Can we really be certain that we are prepared to meet Our Lord? We are plagued with the persistent spiritual problem: we cannot be absolutely certain of salvation at any time in our lives. That is why St. Paul cries out that he works out his salvation in fear and trembling (1 Cor. 9:27; Phil. 2:12).

Those are the spiritual facts of life. It certainly could happen that you and I will NOT be caught up, be raptured, with all those in the state of Sanctifying Grace. We may have to endure the trials and the plagues, the persecution of the time of the troubles.

Therefore it would be very wise for us to consider most carefully the biblical prophecies, the scripture texts which tell us of the eventful ten and a half years prior to the Second Coming. These years, these events, may be your future and mine.

The Rapture should serve as a warning to the Church. It is the first of the great signs to appear in the heavens as recorded in St. John's Apocalypse. In Chapter Twelve of that book, as we have already seen, St. John describes the great PORTENT, the woman

79

clothed with the sun. As I say, we have already discussed this and
the significance of the male son born to that woman. The male son,
that is, the newly elected Pope, was caught up to the throne of God.
In a word, he was raptured. This should, hopefully, serve as a great
sign for those of us unfortunate enough to be left behind. It should
warn us that we do not have much time left before we, too, will
meet the Lord—IN JUDGMENT. We had best amend our lives—in a
hurry!

What, then, is the sequence of events we may be living through?
In the first place it would be wise for us to understand that all the
things we have to discuss in this chapter do not necessarily follow
each other in a nice orderly fashion. The larger order is clear
enough. You will recall that we listed seven major episodes: (1) the
events preceding the Rapture, (2) the Rapture itself, (3) the persecution of the Church, (4) the Russian invasion of Israel, (5) the first
five plagues, (6) Armageddon, (7) the Second Coming. And we have
also indicated to you that a fair number of individual incidents must
be discussed under each of these seven headings.

Not unexpectedly, then, under the general heading of the Persecution of the Church, we will have to take a look at: the consolida-
tion of Anti-Christ's empire, the final form of the ten-nation confederation, the persecution of the Church, the arrival of the "Harlot"
Church, five of the seven seal judgments. We will also give most
careful consideration to the scriptural basis for the time schedule of
all these events.

So—we have studied the *beginnings*, the preliminaries *before*
the Rapture. Now—we have to study many of these *same* events as
they develop *after* the Rapture. They have a continuous and very
natural growth, actually. The Rapture does not halt or interrupt that
continuous development. All the Rapture does is to take the
saints—those in Sanctifying Grace—out of harm's way. Too, it pro-
vides a worldwide warning to all Church members not raptured
that they can still save their souls if they will keep the faith of their
fathers, if they do not give way to the satanic designs, the insidious
blandishments of the evil one, Anti-Christ.

Such being the case, we can pick up where we left off, as it were,
in the chapter dealing with preliminary signs. We saw that a world
leader will arise. It may happen that he will promise and even
secure peace. He will surely be accepted and even acclaimed as a
man of peace, as one capable of bringing a sense of security to a
troubled world. This *before* the Rapture. *After* the Rapture his true
nature will be revealed. He will now move to consolidate his position, his power, his authority.

As Anti-Christ is making his moves, the final formation of the ten nation confederation is also taking place, a union of ten nations originally a part of the old Roman Empire we know so well from our history books.

We have already discussed the various visions granted to the prophet.Daniel. You are, therefore, quite familiar with the vision of the great statue with its head of gold, arms and breast of silver, its legs of iron, and its feet and toes partly of iron and partly of clay (Dan. 2).

The *two* legs of iron represent the two parts of the Roman Empire when it split into the Western and Eastern Empires. The *ten* toes of the statue represent *ten* nations of a future time, and specifically Daniel's end-times, linked together in a somewhat loose confederation, since the symbols of clay and iron are used. (A *confederation* rather than a union or a unity or a oneness because clay and iron do not mix.)

It would seem that Daniel's end-times are our times. If this is so we can expect to see, on the world scene ten nations, five eastern nations and five western nations, joining together in a loosely organized *but* very real federation, ten nations once a part of the old Roman Empire. And—it would seem an altogether likely thing that the European Common Market is the forerunner of this ten nation confederation.

In the book of Revelation, St. John in one of his visions concerning the end-times describes a seven-headed, ten-horned beast arising from the sea. Upon the horns of this beast were ten diadems. The beast was like a leopard, its feet like those of a bear, its mouth like a lion's mouth (Rev. 13:1–2). Various world empires of the past are here represented by the imagery of the leopard, bear and lion.

The seven heads, the ten horns, represent future empires—as does the beast itself, *in toto,* that is. I should add that these were future to St. John, given his vantage point. Now I most certainly wish to keep all options open, but from our vantage point it would certainly seem that we are witnessing the beginning of the fulfillment of this prophecy. The seven heads refer to seven rulers of the latter days. An eighth ruler will arise and exercise control over these seven rulers. This eighth ruler will have worldwide influence, but his actual authority will be over ten nations (or kings, rulers, kingdoms) as represented by the imagery of the ten horns crowned with the ten diadems.

Turn, now, to the book of Daniel, Chapter 8. The picture becomes clear. We can actually visualize the unfolding drama. The ten nations have become a working unity, monetarily, economically, politically. A United States of Europe, in a sense. A well-known leader (who, in reality, is Anti-Christ) has promised, and possibly, achieved an aura, if not an era, of peace and security. He is struggling for control of the ten nation confederation. He achieves success by deceit, defeating three rulers who oppose him. Anti-Christ, therefore, rules three of the ten nations. The other seven nations then join this world-leader, Anti-Christ, quite willingly in an unholy alliance to attain world domination.

This is precisely the scenario Daniel gives us when he tells us of his vision of the four beasts (Dan. 7). The vision of the fourth beast is of particular interest to us. This fourth beast differs from the others; it has *ten* horns. These ten horns are the *ten* nations of which we have been speaking. The symbols are explained for us very clearly by Daniel himself. As he tells us: the fourth beast shall be a fourth kingdom, differing from the ones preceding it. The ten horns are the ten kings (or rulers, those *like* kings, as the Greek phrases it, Rev. 17:12) who shall arise from this kingdom.

Daniel then describes a little horn which arises in the midst of the ten horns and, in so doing, destroys three of the ten horns. As Daniel explains, the little horn represents yet another king who will arise somewhat later than the ten kings and be different from them. Moreover he will put down three of these ten kings.

It is easy to imagine, to visualize these dramatic historical events of the TIME OF THE GREAT TRIBULATION, now rapidly approaching.

At this point I would appeal to all those under thirty-five or forty to please read or review some sort of a brief history of World War II. Those of you who are over thirty-five or forty should remember that period well enough. Please recall the status of Germany and the German people in the 1920's and early 1930's. By reason of the vengeful and horrific treaty imposed upon them at Versailles, the German nation was, quite literally, being starved out of existence. Money was worthless; inflation and depression at one and the same moment caused the price of *one* loaf of bread, just for example, to soar to fifty million marks. Thousands upon thousands of people starved to death. As a result the Communists were able to cause riots and revolts throughout the cities and the universities of Germany. The nation was on the verge of collapse.

At that moment a savior appeared, so it seemed. His name: Adolf Hitler. He brought order out of chaos. A charismatic and forceful speaker, he did, indeed, mesmerize the people. Of course, I suppose people at death's door from the ravages of starvation can be mesmerized rather easily. In any event, the nation suddenly had a future and people responded.

The riots and revolts were brought under control. The economy improved; men were again working. AND there was food to eat. A sense of national pride and national purpose emerged—all under the guidance of this man Adolf Hitler.

In much the same manner, a leader—this next time Anti-Christ—will arise to offer a program of peace and well-being to the European community. He will, in turn, become a dictator, at first exercising a kind of benign overlordship and, thus, extending his authority, power, control over the ten-nation confederation. Much of the world will hail him as a great and glorious leader. He will be the great liberal humanitarian who will, at the start of his reign, achieve peace and prosperity in our times.

Since the European bloc will represent a major force economically and politically in the world, the United States will no longer be the dominant force on the world scene that it once was. (You may not like to admit the fact, but the *fact is* that we have slipped into second place as a world power, even in these present times.) It seems probable that a United States of Europe will assume a more dominant role and the United States of America, while still a great world power, will take a back seat, so far as world leadership is concerned. I make mention of this point now because it seems a possibility that the United States will play a role during the Great Tribulation. Although you won't find any direct scriptural reference to the United States, some symbols used by St. John are suggestive of the United States; quite possibly the United States will be a place of refuge for those who will be persecuted by Anti-Christ.

Yes. Anti-Christ—now that he has achieved control, power—will start to reveal his true colors. He will begin to persecute those Christians left upon the earth after the Rapture; he will try to destroy whatever is left of the Church. And he will, for the most part, succeed. Certainly the Church will be forced underground, at least in those countries dominated by Anti-Christ. By way of example, this will be very similar to the time of the troubles when the English persecuted the Irish and the Catholic Church in Ireland not so very long ago. The Church had to go underground in those days, too. But then the Church survived. Now—under the onslaught of Anti-Christ—it will not, as an organized Church, at least.

The *Tribulation Saints* is the title commonly assigned to those who will die for Our Lord's sake in these perilous times. But of this matter, more later.

First, let us look at the texts from the Scriptures. The point is made clear in St. John's Revelations (Rev. 12). As we have already seen, a "male-son," a newly elected Pope is raptured—plus about one-half of the Church, the members of the Mystical Body of Christ, that is. (*See* Eph. 1:23; Eph. 4:1–16; Eph. 5:30.) Which, by the way, is a point to consider. Some commentators insist that "male-son" refers to Christ. It does! It does in the sense—a *real* sense—that Our Lord is the head, we are the members of one mystical, but nonetheless real, body, the Mystical Body of Christ. At the Rapture the newly elected Vicar of Christ plus Church members in the state of Sanctifying Grace—those of Our Lord's Mystical Body who are spiritually alive—will be caught up to be with Our Lord always, that Our Lord may become all in all. In that sense you could, indeed, say that the phrase "male-son" refers to Our Lord.

As you already know, the dragon (the symbol for Satan, you recall) pursues the woman (the Church) who flees into the desert. The sequence of events is, by now, quite clear. Those Church members left behind at the time of the Rapture will suffer persecution at the hands of Anti-Christ; many will die and many will flee into the desert (a symbolic term meaning a place of refuge) to escape the persecution. Possibly a remnant of the TRUE Church will go underground.

These are the points which are clear:

(1) Anti-Christ will persecute the TRUE Church.

(2) Church members—probably including some Church leaders such as Cardinals, Bishops, some priests and, perhaps, yet another Pope hastily selected to guide the Church in exile—flee to a place prepared for them by God where they will be safe, at least for a while.

(3) Anti-Christ will try to destroy the exiled Church but is prevented from doing so by those peoples and nations not subject to his authority and power.

(4) Whereupon Anti-Christ turns and wages war "against the rest of her off-spring" (Rev. 12:17). St. John explains that these are all those who have kept God's commandments and give testimony to Jesus. The meaning here, so it seems to me, is that *all* Christian Churches will undergo persecution, not just the TRUE Catholic Church; now ALL truly believing and practicing Christians who were unfortunate enough to have missed the Rapture will suffer persecution.

If we are still living upon the earth at this time of the tribulation, St. Matthew tells us that we will be tortured and killed. We will be hated by all the nations. Many of us will falter, betraying and hating one another. Because of the increase of evil, the love of most will grow cold (Mt. 24:9–12).

There are all sorts of ways of torturing a person should one be caught by the forces of Anti-Christ. I should mention a few I suppose, although you usually can read about people being tortured in the daily press. Should you be brought into a prison to be tortured, you could be whipped, I suppose, or beaten with clubs. Then there are various water tortures and electrical tortures. I have read, in *The New York Times*, of some sort of torture whereby pressure is applied to the head until your skull shatters into pieces. Women get raped a lot, but men do too, apparently. If you're a man, they are apt to crush your testicles. Painful thought! And so it goes.

Then, if they are going to kill you, or me, they will behead us. It's a matter of Bible prophecy (Rev. 20:4). So if you miss the Rapture one of the things you can most probably look forward to is being beheaded. Yes, you'll have your head chopped off, if you remain a Christian, that is. So, if you are about to have your head chopped off, the best thing to do would be to make a very sincere act of contrition. They may set up guillotines all over the place. Then they'll just trundle groups of us out to the guillotine and, one by one, fasten our heads in place, release the blade and—plop! there our heads will be—in the basket. Interesting thought! Shades of the French Revolution! Wow!

In any case, St. Mark offers some interesting details. He tells us that we can expect to be handed over to the courts, to be beaten in the synagogues (lynch mobs?), arraigned before governors and kings (Mk. 13:9). Worse yet, brother will deliver up brother to death, fathers will give over their children to death, children will rise against parents and have them put to death.

Such things cannot happen, you say. They *have* happened; they *are* happening; they *will* happen. Please, believe me! The prophecy *will be fulfilled!* We will be hounded, tortured, put to death. But if we endure these days and maintain our faith, we will be saved.

And, indeed, it may be that you, or I, might escape the headsman and languish in prison for a while. We might also escape and go underground. These things are also a possibility. In any case, we will not have to worry about what to say or how to defend ourselves. In St. Luke's gospel, for example, Our Lord says that we will not have to worry about how to answer our accusers or those who are trying us. We will bear testimony to Our Lord and He will tell us what to say: "I will give you a mouth and wisdom which none of your adversaries will be able to withstand or contradict" (Lk. 21:13–15).

Of course, Our Lord adds the somewhat sobering thought that we ought to pray always that we may be accounted worthy to escape all

these trials and tribulations (Lk. 21:36). We've alluded to this before, somewhere along the line. It bears repeating. If Our Lord says
that we ought to lead lives of prayer, that we should always be
prepared to greet Him at the moment of the Rapture, thus escaping
the dreadful trials that will follow upon that great warning sign, I
am most willing to take *Him* at *His* word. I only hope He finds *me*
prepared.

If we are alive at this time of the tribulation, and remain alive
during it, we will also have to endure the insidious onslaughts of
the ANTI-POPE.

Oh, yes! The Anti-Pope!

Perhaps I had better explain, just a bit. If you will open your
Bibles to the book of Revelation, Chapters 12 and 13, you will see
what I'm talking about. In the first part of Chapter 12, the red
dragon with two horns and seven heads is menacing the woman
about to give birth. We have already discussed the meaning of the
symbols here. The red dragon is Satan, the woman is the Church. At
the moment that the Rapture occurs and the male-son (a newly
elected Pope, as we have already indicated) is caught up to God
and God's throne, Satan is cast out of his place in the heavens and
thrust down upon the earth by Michael and his angels.

Thereupon, Satan immediately attacks the Church. This attack,
judging by St. John's description, is a visible, tangible, physical
assault. To attack the Church in a visible, tangible, physical manner, Satan himself will have to become visible, tangible, physical.
In a word, Satan will need a visible, tangible, physical body. And a
power base from which he can launch his attack upon the Church.

I'm sure you see what I'm leading up to. Satan will take possession of the body of Anti-Christ. Again, I am not saying this of my-
self. I am simply paraphrasing the scenario provided by St. John. If
you read along with me, you'll see what I mean. All I'm doing now
is paraphrasing the first part of Chapter 13 of the book of Revelation.

Please notice the beast which arises from the sea. The description of the dragon and the beast are almost the same. Both have ten
horns and seven heads. The only difference is that the dragon has
seven diadems upon its seven heads whereas the beast has ten
diadems upon its ten horns. The crowns upon the heads of the
dragon simply represent the power Satan has always exercised over
nations. (He is the Prince of this world, remember. When Satan
tempted Our Lord in the desert, he offered Our Lord all the kingdoms of the world. This would not have been much of a temptation

unless all the kingdoms of the world were really Satan's to offer.) The crowns upon the horns of the beast represent the kingdoms over which Anti-Christ will exercise authority.

Now—at the time of the Rapture, the beast receives a mortal wound. This mortal wound is a sword wound (Rev. 13:3; Rev. 13:14). These two facts are clear. Just how it happens that Anti-Christ receives a mortal wound, we are not told. As can happen with any well-known personality or world leader, perhaps some sort of assassination attempt is made upon his life. This we do not know.

In any case it *is clear* that Anti-Christ receives a death blow. This mortal wound is healed and Anti-Christ is brought back to life; Satan gives to Anti-Christ his own power and throne and authority. Satan, then, very obviously inhabits the body of Anti-Christ, in some way revives Anti-Christ and the world witnesses what appears to be a resurrection. This causes the "whole world" to follow after the beast. The "whole world" worships the dragon and the beast. (I must add the explanatory note: the "whole world" means the sphere of Anti-Christ's influence. The phrase does not include Russia and her allies, the "King of the South" and his allies, the "Kings of the East" and the "Great Eagle." *See* Dan. 11:5; Rev. 12:14; Rev. 16:12; Ezek., Chapter 39.)

Again—*two* personalities are involved. Satan has his personality; Anti-Christ retains his personality. Now Anti-Christ is imbued with the spirit of Satan. From this point forward Satan is Anti-Christ, Anti-Christ is Satan. We have now a satanic duo.

But—as you should realize, Satan desires to be God. But God is Trinity, a tri-une God. You may be sure that Satan will try to be the tri-une God also. And he does. A third personality is added to the infamous and evil duo now leading the world astray. Following along with St. John's description of world events right after the Rapture, a *second* beast arises from the earth. This beast has *two* horns and speaks like a *dragon*.

Let us stop for a moment and consider the imagery, the symbolism here. It is fascinating.

(1) A beast—one who is evil.

(2) Having two horns like a ram (i.e., a male sheep)—one representing Our Lord, the slain Lamb.

(3) Who speaks like a dragon—one who is an agent of the Devil.

(4) This beast *leads* the earth's inhabitants *to worship* an idol of the first beast.

We have, therefore, a religious leader, who *has* and *exercises* real authority and is able to lead people in worship, one who seems to stand in the place of, seems to represent Our Lord, yet one who is evil and speaks as a representative of Satan.

But—who is a religious leader who stands in place of, represents Our Lord, the slain Lamb? Who leads the earth's inhabitants in worship? Who exercises such enormous authority that the earth's inhabitants accept such authority, such leadership in offering worship?

A Pope.

Who is evil, who can speak as Satan's agent in this position of a world renowned religious leader?

An Anti-Pope!

Of course!

Have there been Anti-Popes in the history of the Church? You know the answer to that one as well as I do. Of course there have been Anti-Popes. There will be again! As a matter of fact three Anti-Popes, men who claim they are the Pope, exist at the present moment and apparently have some sort of following. (Some have even suggested that the name of the Anti-Pope at the time of the persecution of the TRUE Church will be Gregory the Seventeenth.)

There will be an Anti-Pope, regardless of name. As St. John describes it for us in Chapter 13 of Revelation, Anti-Pope will speak with the authority of the first beast. Therefore we can know that Anti-Pope is working, hand in glove, with Anti-Christ and Satan. Anti-Pope is able to and does induce the world and all its inhabitants to worship the first beast, that is Anti-Christ who is also Satan. In a word Anti-Pope will lead the world in the worship of Satan.

If you feel slightly bewildered by all of this, be reassured. So do I. As we have said earlier. Once these events *start* to gel, *everything* will move *very quickly*. How, then, has all this come to pass? Let us stop, back up, and take another look, step by step:

(1) A very difficult papal election has occurred.

(2) A Pope has been elected—and immediately raptured.

(3) The allies of Anti-Christ, both civil and ecclesiastic, will force those faithful to the TRUE Church underground.

(4) Those faithful to the TRUE Church have hastily elected another TRUE Pope who flees into the wilderness. (This flight is described as happening by means of the two wings of the great eagle. Could it be that the TRUE Pope will take refuge in the United States, or with United States aid? This, by the way, may be the one reference to the United States in Scripture. Too, I would add that Anti-Pope seems to imply the existence of a TRUE Pope. Such a true

Pope would not be prominent since he would be a refugee somewhere. It is a thought, in any case.)

(5) The forces of Anti-Christ/Satan have seized control of the
Church in Rome, control of the Vatican.

(6) The forces of Anti-Christ elect a Pope, a FALSE Pope, an
Anti-Pope.

(7) Now, Satan, Anti-Christ, and Anti-Pope really join forces, and
as a satanic *trio* work their will upon the world.

A satanic trio.

A satanic trinity! Satan now falsely emulates the true God he
wishes to be. He has managed to create, however falsely, a trinity,
an evil force of unity in three personalities, an evil trinity. Thus it is
that Satan mocks the very inner life of the Godhead, the love of
Father for Son and Son for Father, of Father and Son for Holy
Spirit, of Holy Spirit for Father and Son. And even as the inner life
of the TRUE God is love, so must the inner life of the false god be
hate.

Hate! Hatred now rules supreme in the world. And now mankind
will experience the full fury of satanic hatred such as never yet has
been experienced in the world before or ever will be in the ages to
come.

And, now, the HARLOT church. If the TRUE Church—what is left
of it, that is—exists in exile, what can we say of the False church
which exists in Rome (i.e., Mystery Babylon, of which more later)?
It is clearly the Harlot church of St. John's Revelations. This false
church, headed by Anti-Pope, leads the world's inhabitants in the
worship of Anti-Christ AND, also in offering worship to the idol of
Anti-Christ. Anti-Pope, the false prophet, works signs and wonders
in the sight of men. He can, for example, make fire come down from
the heavens (Rev. 13:13). Thus, he induces others, by such deceit
and trickery, to worship Anti-Christ and the idol of Anti-Christ.

So—the Rapture has occurred. The main characters of the fateful
ten and one-half years between the Rapture and the Second Coming are in place. Anti-Christ, who before the Rapture seemed to be
a savior bringing peace and security to the world, is now indwelt by
Satan; Anti-Pope is ruling over the "Harlot" church. The remnant
of TRUE Church members is being persecuted, horribly tortured,
put to death by beheading. TRUE Church members in the state of
sanctifying grace have been raptured (Eph. 4:30). It is those who
were, therefore, not raptured, who are enduring the persecution,
the torture, the beheading I just mentioned.

Of course, this is, in reality, a Divine favor. Indeed, it would be wise to remember that all that is going on is under God's control. All things work for His purpose and according to His plan. Anyone raptured in the state of mortal sin would end up in hell—which is not the purpose of the Rapture. Having been left behind, they (for all I know, we) will now have a chance to save their (our) souls and enter into Heaven by suffering martyrdom for Our Lord's sake.

Before turning to a consideration of the seal judgments (Revelation, Chapters 6 and 7 and also Chapter 8, Verses 1 and 2), Divine judgments which occur during the first three and a half years of Anti-Christ's reign, judgments which affect all nations and peoples, let me reiterate: it is the fact that ALL the forces for evil which we have been discussing are operative, either together or sequentially, within the same time frame, as it were, which should alert us to the fact that *the moment of Judgment* is upon us.

Forces disruptive of human society have been alive and well and functional throughout the past ages of man—*but separately*. "The secret force of lawlessness is already at work . . ." (2 Thess. 2:7). Now in our present age these events are happening or beginning to happen pretty much at the same time. THAT is the clue.

The Apostasy, for example, will herald the advent of the "harlot" church. The apostate church will teach probably quite clearly and distinctly, a faith and a moral code which will differ markedly from the Faith of Our Fathers. The trigger for this "formal" apostasy may well be the "formal" rejection by many Church leaders and members of the traditional Christian moral code governing the sexual mores of Church members, at the very least.

I must make mention of a few worldwide phenomena with which we will be afflicted. On a worldwide scale abortions will abound, true of our present age. The use of drugs will be a worldwide phenomenon, true of our present age; this, in turn, is related to the witchcraft so prevalent in our days. In the Greek, *pharmakeus* is a person dealing in drugs and specifically an enchanter, magician, a sorcerer (i.e., those involved in witchcraft or the worship of the Devil) (Rev. 9:21). Satanism is widespread.

Among other things, I should mention famines which, Our Lord tells us, will be widespread. Only five years ago there was a "Green Revolution." It was thought famine (and the disease resulting from famine) would be conquered. *Now*—five years later—there is worldwide famine. Ten thousand people a day are dying of famine.

Pestilence, plague follow upon famine, of course.

As far as pestilence is concerned, we are experiencing in our day a worldwide epidemic of venereal disease. This is a plague of our modern world since this disease is now out of control and the famed penicillin cure no longer cures.

So we *are,* now, experiencing widespread famine and pestilence (Lk. 21:11).

Then there is fornication. This is the order of day, in these our times, of course.

Then, of course, there is homosexuality which is very widespread today and quite openly practiced (Is. 3:9). Of course, in ancient times fornication and/or homosexuality was tied in with the worship of idols. Such sexual activity is quite prevalent in today's business world (to say nothing of the world of government!) in order to achieve advancement, position, better pay and so forth. So I suppose you could say that what went on in ancient times goes on today.

St. John, in Chapter 2 of Revelation, Verse 6, inveighs against the Nicolaitans who went about fornicating with anybody whenever or wherever they could, but with one interesting variation. Apparently they dressed themselves in animal skins, then set about the business of fornicating. Rather strange.

In any case, they (the Nicolaitans) would feel pretty much at home in today's world.

Let's see. What else is going on worldwide? As far as I can see everything is going on worldwide. Murder, certainly. Thievery, lying, adultery, naturally. Drugs, abortion. Disowning, dishonoring parents and elders; complete disregard of God's laws regarding—anything. (*See* 2 Tim. 3:1–9 and Rev. 9:21.)

So it goes. What can I tell you? It is not a pretty picture. But it is a true picture of our times. Put ALL the pieces together and they spell out: THE LATTER DAYS!

During the first three and a half years of Anti-Christ's reign God will strive to bring people to their senses, to get people to repent of their sins, to fall to their knees in prayer and supplication, asking forgiveness.

God will do this by sending upon all peoples and nations a number of judgments indicative of the Divine Wrath. These judgments are symbolized by St. John as a series of seals. Let me describe the scene for you and explain the imagery.

St. John tells us (Revelation, Chapters 5 and 6) that he saw, in a vision, a scroll in the hand of the One seated upon the throne. This scroll is sealed with seven seals. No one is found worthy to break open these seals, whereupon St. John weeps much (as he himself phrases it).

However, one of the elders tells him not to weep, the Lion of the tribe of Judah, the Root of David, has conquered. Therefore he can open the scroll, break open the seven seals.

The Lamb then appears—in the next scene, as it were—and takes the scroll. This slain Lamb—Our Lord, of course—receives the adulation of the elders, of the myriad upon myriads of angels. Our Lord then proceeds to break open the first of the seals.

Before going any further, I think I had better offer an explanatory note or two. The opening of seals by a Lamb who has been slain may seem somewhat strange to us in modern day America. Such imagery would not seem strange or odd to St. John or to early Church members, especially if they were of Jewish background.

When the nation Israel took possession of the land—their land, the Promised Land—certain norms were established regarding the distribution of that land and maintaining an even distribution among the people. Thus, a man, and his family, was given a piece of land, of property. This man could sell the property, or otherwise dispose of it. However, the bill of sale was really only a lease because it automatically expired in the year of Jubilee (every fiftieth year) and then the ownership of the land reverted to the original owner.

If a man sold his property or lost it in some way and his children were, on that account, disinherited, the land could be bought back by a kinsman who could pay the *purchase price*. This could be done at any time. The land would then be returned to its proper owners. The kinsman who did such a thing was called a *redeemer*, and the act of returning the land to its rightful owners was known as *redemption* and the entire transaction was known as the "redemption of the purchased possession" (Lev. 25:23–31). Now such a transaction was, quite naturally, recorded in writing, on a scroll, again quite naturally. This record was rolled up, sealed, and delivered to the original owner, or to his heir. The kinsman or the redeemer, the one who had paid the purchase price, was the one who could break open the seals. The open book gave the redeemer the right to repossess the land; it was the redeemer who would break open the seals (or, as we would phrase it today, "burn the mortgage").

The imagery used by St. John should now be reasonably clear to you. Our Lord has inherited all things from the Father. (We are co-heirs with Our Lord by reason of adoption.) However, Satan is in possession of the world, even though the "purchase price" has been paid. Our Lord, our kinsman, has redeemed the world at the

price of his own blood (1 Pt. 1:18–20). The world should be returned to its original owner. But Satan refuses to leave. Therefore
the seals will be broken open; Our Lord will now proceed, with the
authority of the opened book, to claim the earth as His own.

Basically St. John does what Daniel did, and Ezekiel as well. He
draws word pictures. While he uses apocalyptic imagery to do this,
nevertheless he is simply drawing pictures, in short sequences,
scene by scene (or frame by frame, if you like). Therefore, in the
first place, it is helpful to visualize the characters as they are described. I do not deny the fact that guidance is needed and most
helpful, but with a thoughtful consideration of the details given us
we should be able to get at the *personalities,* at the *characteristics*
of the people being described. PLEASE NOTE!! *Personality* type;
characteristics of the personality type. By NO stretch of the imagination can we or dare we say that St. John's descriptions apply to
specific persons, a person, such as Napoleon or Hitler, for example.
Just such interpretation has discredited Bible prophecy over the
centuries.

After the fact, once the prophecy has been fulfilled then—and
only then—can we be certain of the person or persons involved.
Before the fact we had best deal with what St. John (or the other
prophets) gives us: descriptions of personality types.

Dealing, thus, with pictures, with scenes, with personalities, we
have, quite clearly, the ingredients for a motion picture in the classic style. Directing of great brilliance would be required. To convey the inner meaning, the real message hidden in the external
trapping of words, a group of extraordinary actors and actresses
would be needed. What I'm trying to do is to get you to use your
imagination in a controlled manner. The scenes written down by
St. John, by Daniel, by Ezekiel are of REAL but FUTURE events; it
seems that these FUTURE events are starting to come true in our
times; to describe these REAL events, the authors use visual and
unusual IMAGERY; as an aid to grasping the reality of the events it is
helpful to see them as scene following upon scene, in the fluid
flowing style of the motion picture; as an aid to grasping the real-
ness of the leading personalities involved in these events it is helpful to see them as *real* people, which they are and will be. (For
example, Anti-Pope will NOT be some intellectual personification.
Anti-Pope *will be* a very real man, and, at the start, probably an
astute politician, and a very likable person, if you are not one of his
victims.)

And the events these persons will be identified with, that these
persons will be responsible for, will trigger, will be very real, too.

To continue, then, with our discussion of the seal judgments. The first four of these judgments are described by way of a very, very famous image, one with which you are all familiar: the Four Horsemen of the Apocalypse. Dread figures, they march over the face of the earth. In that first image, a white horse, the rider comes forth conquering and to conquer. CONQUEST. By fair means or foul, Anti-Christ will seek to extend his kingdom. It is easy to imagine, is it not? We have seen it so often. The imperialism of the Roman emperors extending their rule over the then known world; the imperialism of Napoleon as he extends his rule over much of Europe and Russia; the imperialism of the British Empire extending its rule around the globe; Hitler's imperialism in the late 1930's and early 1940's of our present age. So Anti-Christ will seek to extend his rule over Europe and adjacent near-Eastern countries, and also, perhaps, into Africa and South America. But as he seeks dominion, by diplomatic ploys, the promise of peace which he holds forth, the second seal is opened. Now a red horse and rider marches over the face of the earth, the red horse and rider who bring war upon the earth. WAR. Thus it is clear that as Anti-Christ seeks to rule over the nations, some offer resistance and war breaks out. Nations for Anti-Christ will do battle with those nations opposing Anti-Christ. (Just how these nations will be aligned is not at all clear and it is best not to conjecture about this.) Suffice it to know that wars will occur. Even as Napoleon was successful for a time, even as Hitler was successful for a time, so Anti-Christ will be successful for a time. History helps us to visualize the sequence of events, because we have had the same exact sequence of events in the past.

And the forces attendant upon war? Famine, hunger, inflation, black market, you name it. These, all these, are unleashed at the breaking of the third seal. And, now, a third horse and rider, this time a black horse, join the other two. And now the three horsemen march over the face of the earth. CONQUEST BY DECEIT, WAR, FAMINE.

Here in the United States we have never quite experienced the full impact of modern warfare. I remember the black market and the rationing of World War II, as do many of you. But I was still in high school during that war and never experienced the horrors of the battlefield. This, too, would be true for many of you. No, for all our involvement in the two world wars, to many of us total warfare is something foreign and unknown. I realize that we are feeling the aftereffects of the Vietnam war. Inflation-depression economy is eroding the fabric of our present society. But, as yet, what we have experienced and are experiencing on the "home front," as they say, is little or nothing of the devastating destruction which is modern warfare. Many of us here in the United States will have to put our imaginations to work to capture the horrifying feel of, the stupefying emotional and physical impact that will be our future should we be alive at the time of the seal judgments.

Call to mind some of the more realistic war movies you may have seen. What you experience vicariously in the movie you will experience in reality. That will be YOU fleeing invading armies with just the clothing on your back, your home destroyed, your family torn apart, your children missing. That will be YOU suffering the dreadful effects of acute hunger and starvation. That will be YOU trying to get some clothing or a blanket on the black market.

Or, if you can, call to mind and try to visualize, *really* feel the famine, the hunger, the degradation that people suffered in the early 1930's, the years of the great depression.

Then, *maybe,* you will begin to get the feel of, get a grip on what is going to happen to YOU at the time of the seal judgments.

And the fourth horse and its rider. DEATH. With the breaking of the fourth seal, the fourth horseman—sickly green—joins the other three. Death has entered the picture. And many will die, as many as a fourth of all the people of the earth (Rev. 6:8). And how will one-quarter of the earth's population die? By the sword (the weapons of war), by famine, by pestilence and—strange as it may sound—by wild beasts of the earth.[1] With society broken down, civilians without weapons, wild animals can take their toll. When there is a great scarcity of food, do not wolves, bears come out of the forest by night seeking human prey? Where there is lack of food, do not the great savage cats, as the tiger, become man-hunters? Yes, they do, even in our own highly sophisticated times. To say nothing of cannibalism!

The Four Horsemen of the Apocalypse march across the face of the earth. Dread figures!

A motion picture I saw some years ago, named "Fraulein Doktor," I believe, comes to mind. The film is a classic spy story of World War I. Fraulein Doktor is a brilliant German spy who causes the French and the British a good bit of trouble. The plot, then, is in the classic mold of the genre. But the film truly captures the *feel* of war, the *horror* of war and its consequences. It is surely the way in which this movie is filmed and edited which makes it a brilliant classic.

---

[1] It is quite possible that packs of rabid dogs will be attacking human beings. It is, then, quite possible that a rabies epidemic will kill many people.

Those scenes—in black and white—which show the use of poison gas in that first world war are shocking. The gas, a French invention for use against the Germans, stolen by Fraulein Doktor for German use against the French, is released upon the battlefield. Mists of poison gas roll across the desolate, devastated landscape, and into the trenches, and men fall dead. Those who live flee from the trenches, screaming, their lungs afire from inhaled poison gas.

And then—slowly—slowly—in horrifying fashion, out of the mists of gas great monsters seem to appear. Dark masked figures astride great dark and hooded beasts. Slowly—the dark, frightening, unrecognizable figures march across the landscape. With a start you realize—these are men wearing dark protective clothing and gas masks astride horses cloaked in dark protective trappings and fitted out with gas masks. Slowly—relentlessly—these monstrous creatures, dread figures, these horsemen march across the bleak surface of the earth, coming out of the darkness to wreak their vengeance upon those who stand helplessly in their path. They sweep all before them.

Horrifying vision, but a real one, and it gives some little notion of the powerful imagery of St. John; the Four Horsemen of the Apocalypse!

The fifth seal is then opened and St. John presents us with yet another scene. It reminds us that even as the false peace, and the wars, famine, devastation are affecting many of the world's people, so those who are Christian are also undergoing martyrdom. St. John sees the souls of all those who have been killed for the Word of God and for the witness they have borne. Not yet united in body and soul, although saved, these martyrs cry out, asking Our Lord how much longer they must wait. They are given a white robe and are told to wait just a bit longer, until the time when the number of their fellow servants and their brothers is completed, those to be slain, even as they had been slain.

There is more. The book of Revelation is a bloody one, no question. Before turning to that sixth seal, however, I want to digress, ever so briefly, and give the reasoning which underlies the *timing* we are following, the reason we know that ten and one-half years is the correct time span between the Rapture and the Second Coming. I should also like to tell you why we know that the first events of this period will occur over a period of three and one-half years, the time of the first five seals, the time of the great tribulation.

Firstly, St. John gives us the time element, the span of years during which Anti-Christ will have authority over all peoples, races, languages, nations and will wage war on God's people. The time period here is forty-two months (Rev 13:5–8). Forty-two months is three and a half years. Furthermore the true Church will experience the hardships of exile and martyrdom for "a time and times and half a time." Modern translations render this phrase as "a year and for two and a half years more" which is precisely what it means, three and a half years (Rev. 12:14).

Secondly, the sixth seal is broken. This starts the invasion of Israel by Gog and Magog (i.e., Russia). (We will discuss this event in detail in the next chapter. For the moment, please bear with me; Israel *will be* invaded by Russia.) This will occur over a *very short* period of time because Russia will be severely defeated and crushed by Divine intervention. (PLEASE NOTE! This invasion is NOT Armageddon.[1]) We are told that the persecution of God's people (i.e., the True Church) will last forty-two months. THEN it stops. The scene of the fifth seal shows us the martyrs in heaven soon to be joined by their fellow servants and brothers, and we are told, in Revelation, Chapter 7, that at the time of the Russian invasion or shortly thereafter God's servants are to be sealed with the seal of the living God so that they will be kept free of harm. Therefore—three and a half years have elapsed by the time the persecution of the True Church comes to an end. And it is toward the end of this three and a half years that the Russian invasion occurs.

Now—in Ezekiel, Chapter 39, we are given an account of the Russian invasion. Ezekiel, in that 39th chapter, prophesies that the Russian army will be soundly defeated and, thereafter, the people of Israel will use the weapons of war for *seven* years as fuel, presumably until Armageddon ends this practice, "for seven years they [the Israelites] shall make fires with them [the weapons of war]" (Ezek. 39:9).

Furthermore, in Daniel's famous vision of the seventy weeks (Dan. 9:24–27), we are informed that Anti-Christ will make a firm treaty with the Israeli government "for one week," that is, for seven years. Halfway through those seven years Anti-Christ will break the treaty. He will abolish sacrifice and oblation in the Temple and he will set up the "abomination of desolation" in the temple. This idol, of Anti-Christ himself probably, will repose in the temple and many people will offer sacrifices to it, worship it, for "half the week," that is, for three and a half years, until "the ruin that is decreed is poured out upon the horror," until the moment of Armageddon.

[1] See Appendix IV.

(I should explain that Daniel was granted a prophetic vision of salvation history, a history taking place over a period of "seventy weeks." Actually a literal translation of the Hebrew text is a period of "seventy sevens." The "sevens" could refer to days or to years, depending on context. A week of days is seven days; a "week" of years is seven years. The seventh day was a day of rest; the seventh year was a year of rest, especially for the land. That is the origin of our word sabbatical, the phrase sabbatical year. So, in Daniel, the "seventy sevens" refer to seventy sevens of years, as is obvious from the context.)

Now—the events I have just described as occurring over a seven year period occur *during the same time period* as the trumpet/bowl judgments. (We will be discussing the trumpet/bowl judgments at great length very shortly. However, I should explain the trumpets and bowls are the symbols used by St. John to describe the *same* judgments, seven in all, that God will visit upon mankind as punishments for sin, but also to try to bring all men to repentance that they may—*willingly* and *freely*—save their immortal souls. These trumpet/bowl judgments occur over a *seven* year period and during the same *seven* year period which begins when Anti-Christ enters into a firm treaty with the government of Israel, then breaks the treaty, establishes worship of himself in the Temple and which ends with the battle of Armageddon.) [1] I must also note that a gap exists between seal six and trumpet/bowl one. Seal seven is "silence the space of a half hour." This apparently is a very short period of time. Thus our timing must always be approximate.

Now—the trumpet/bowl judgments *follow* the seal judgments (Rev. 8:1–6).

So—

(1) The seal judgments take 3½ years.

(2) The trumpet/bowl judgments take 7 years.

(3) Therefore—the time span between the Rapture and the moment of Armageddon and Our Lord's Second Coming is 10½ years. [2]

I believe this is a quite reasonably clear chronology of the events of the latter days.

I should warn you, I suppose, that many, many commentators push all these events into a period of seven years. Thus in many books you will find that the time span which separates the Rapture and the Second Coming is seven years. Those authors who compress all the events of which we have spoken into seven years think

[1] See Appendix V.
[2] For a detailed discussion of this problem see Appendix V.

that the Russian invasion of Israel and the battle of Armageddon are one and the same event, or two parts of one single event. They think that the events described in Revelation, Chapter 6, Verses 12–16; the fifth trumpet/bowl judgment described in Revelation, Chapter 9, Verses 1–3 and Chapter 16, Verses 10–11; and the seventh trumpet/bowl judgment described in Revelation, Chapter 11, Verse 19 and Chapter 16, Verses 17–21 are one and the same event or different descriptions of the same event.

The truth of the matter is that three quite separate and distinct events, and occurring at quite distinct times, are being described in the book of Revelation. St. John lists *three* distinct occasions when there will be violent earthquakes, when the sun will be darkened, the powers of heaven shaken, when the stars will fall from the heavens and the sky itself disappear as it were. There will be lightning flashes and peals of thunder and giant hailstones the *size of a talent* (talantiaia is the Greek) (Rev. 16:21) hailstones about the size of a bocci ball and weighing about six pounds, therefore, will come crashing down on men from the sky.

The three times when these violent upheavals in nature will occur during the latter days are:

(1) The Russian invasion of Israel.

(2) The fifth trumpet/bowl judgment.

(3) The seventh trumpet/bowl judgment, or Armageddon.

That these are three distinct and separate events is confirmed by the prophet Joel.

(1) Joel, Chapter 2, Verses 10 and 20: the sun and moon are darkened, the stars withhold their brightness; this will be at the time when the northerner (i.e., the Russians) is removed from the land of Israel; *then* the Spirit will be poured out upon all mankind and old men shall dream dreams and young men shall see visions. [Joel's prophecy (Joel 3:1–3) of the outpouring of the Spirit was *partially* fulfilled at the time of Pentecost (Acts 2:17–21); *complete* fulfillment awaits the latter days and the Day of the Lord of which Joel prophesies.]

(2) Then, in Joel, Chapter 3, Verses 3 and 4, we are told that *"at the coming of the day of the Lord"* (or as the Jerusalem Bible translates the phrase: *"before* the day of Yahweh dawns, that great and terrible day"*) wonders will be worked in the heavens and the earth, "blood, fire, and columns of smoke; the sun will be turned to darkness, and the moon to blood." This event corresponds to the fifth trumpet/bowl judgment of St. John's Revelation.

(3) And still a *third* time, Joel (4:12–16) prophesies that the sun and the moon will be darkened and the stars will withhold their

brightness, the heavens and the earth will quake when the nations have gathered in the Valley of Jehoshaphat, the place of final judgment, the valley of decision. This is the time of, the actual moment of, Armageddon. (*See* Mt. 24:29 which also describes this.)

We have, then, in Joel and in Revelation *three* distinct events and these events occur during the final *seven* years of the ten and a half year span we label the latter days or the end-time or the Day of the Lord.

If I miss the Rapture, I have just described my future. If you miss the Rapture I have just described your future. That future is far from pleasant. I beg of you: be prepared. I know I am trying, struggling to be always prepared for the Rapture. I don't know how successful I am being, but you can bet your bottom dollar on it, I am trying and I am going to keep on trying. I can only hope that my description of what the future WILL BE will help you to keep trying and struggling to be prepared for the Rapture, too.

VI

The Russians Are Coming!
The Russians Are Coming!

The action moves swiftly. Inexorably, relentlessly, the drama builds to its inevitable climax. The satanic trinity, Anti-Christ indwelt by Satan and Anti-Pope imbued with Satan's spirit control the ten nation confederation and now seek to extend their influence and exercise their authority over neighboring nations and, indeed, the entire world. We can learn a lesson from history here. Hitler's Germany, Napoleon's France were prototypes of Anti-Christ's empire.

And the setting for this drama of the latter days? Rome. Anti-Christ's capital will be Rome; Anti-Pope will reign, of course, from the Vatican. St. John is quite clear about this. In Revelation, Chapter 17, St. John speaks of the harlot who sits upon the seven hills and the harlot is, among other things, the great city. It is, of course, an established fact that THE city of seven hills is Rome. And it is an established historical fact that the euphemism for Rome in St. John's day was Babylon. The fact that St. John calls Rome Babylon causes a great deal of difficulty for many *present day* commentators. I do not understand why. St. Peter, for example, writing his first epistle from Rome (an established historical fact), says he is writing from Babylon (1 Pt. 5:13). Moreover, we do precisely the same thing today. If I were writing an article on cities in the United States and used such euphemisms as Fun City, Sin City, and Windy City, even the Big Apple, everyone would know that I was referring to New York City, Los Angeles, and Chicago. The one difficult euphemism would be Sin City. That title has been used to describe a number of cities because so many cities in the United States vie for it. However, if I qualify my descriptive titles with such phrases as City of Skyscrapers, City of Smog and Freeways, then it is clear that I mean New York City and Los Angeles. St. John does exactly

101

the same thing when he describes Rome as Babylon, the city of seven hills. Without question he means Rome.

Rome will be Anti-Christ's headquarters; Vatican City will be Anti-Pope's headquarters. I hope I am not shocking any Catholic readers. But there have been a number of Anti-Popes in the long history of the Roman Catholic Church and there will be another Anti-Pope, quite possibly in the near future. I'm sorry, but that's the way it is, or will be rather.

Have we any well-known ecclesiastical precedent, someone relatively well known to most of us to serve as an example? I think, perhaps, such a person would be the infamous Cardinal Richelieu. He could well serve as the example. Here we have the high Church dignitary working to serve his own interests (Power) and the interests of the state (France). I'm sure most of us are quite familiar with that highly romantic novel *The Three Musketeers* by Alexandre Dumas, pere. If you haven't read the book, you most certainly have seen the movie versions of that story, the Musketeers riding to the rescue of someone in distress—the Queen, perhaps, her honor threatened by the evil Cardinal and the Cardinal's men.

Now—turn the evil Cardinal into Anti-Pope who is working, hand in glove, with Anti-Christ for his own interests (Power) and the interests of the state (Anti-Christ's empire). I think this should give you a picture, not too far off the mark, of what is in the near future. Dumas wrote a romantic, adventure-filled novel. The future events of which we are speaking will be far from romantic, nor do I think you would consider them adventuresome. The future, now dawning upon us, will be living hell for those who will suffer torture, imprisonment, and death at the hands of Anti-Christ and Anti-Pope.

You may be wondering why I am describing Anti-Pope in such a manner. I do because St. John does. Thus, the second beast exercises all the authority of the first beast in its presence (Rev. 13:11–17). Anti-Pope, then, is the right-hand man, the minister of Anti-Christ. More, Anti-Pope causes the earth's inhabitants to worship Anti-Christ. Anti-Pope, you realize, cannot cause this to happen instantly. He has to work at it and bring it to pass by degrees. You will recall that we discussed the mortal wound received by Anti-Christ, the fact that Satan took possession of Anti-Christ's body and, thereby, was the cause of what seemed to be a resurrection, Anti-Christ restored to life. The whole world wondered at this and certainly many people became followers of Anti-Christ at that point.

It is clear, from the description St. John gives us, that Anti-Pope will have been actively engaged in promoting this particular deception and the interests of Anti-Christ in general.

Keep in mind, however, that even as Anti-Pope is working to enhance and to strengthen and to spread the kingdom and the power and the glory of Anti-Christ, so he is working most assiduously, feverishly, to establish and consolidate his own interests. Judging by St. John's description, Anti-Pope is the minister of finance or, if you prefer, secretary of the treasury. He is the man in charge of buying, of selling, of commerce, of finance. He will exercise a rigid control over those who wish to engage in business activities, at least those within the confines of Anti-Christ's empire. He will have such people marked with the name, or the number which stands for the name, of Anti-Christ (Rev. 13:17). Within that empire everyone is marked. Christians who refuse the mark will not even be able to buy groceries, will starve to death, or beg from the burghers in order to stay alive. Some sort of credit card economy is implied. Those living in distant lands, far from the borders of Anti-Christ's empire might not be so marked. I'm sure such merchants would be allowed to trade with merchants living within the empire, should it suit the purposes of Anti-Christ or Anti-Pope. By the same token, many foreign merchants might accept the mark of Anti-Christ in order to trade within the empire.

In addition to his duties as Chancellor of the Exchequer, Anti-Pope will reign over a one-world religion (much to the consternation of Ecumenists around the world, I suppose). This one-world religion is a false religion and the "harlot" religion St. John describes in Revelation, Chapter 17, Verses 1–6.

"Then one of the seven angels who had the seven bowls came and said to me, 'Come, I will show you the judgment of the great harlot who is seated upon many waters, with whom the kings of the earth have committed fornication, and with the wine of whose fornication the dwellers on earth have become drunk.' And he carried me away in the Spirit into a wilderness, and I saw a woman sitting on a scarlet beast which was full of blasphemous names, and it had seven heads and ten horns. The woman was arrayed in purple and scarlet, and bedecked with gold and jewels and pearls, holding in her hand a golden cup full of abominations and the impurities of her fornication; and on her forehead was written a name of mystery: 'Babylon the great, mother of harlots and of earth's abominations.' And I saw the woman, drunk with the blood of the saints and the blood of the martyrs of Jesus." RSV

There we have the harlot church. First, let's take a look at the symbols. As was the case in Chapter 12 of Revelation, the woman represents the Church. And the woman also represents the city of Rome. Why do we speak of the two-fold symbolism? St. John says of the woman that "she is the great city which has sovereignty over

the kings of the earth" (Rev. 17:18). In Chapter 18, Verse 9, St. John
also says of this city (which he calls Babylon which is, as we have
shown, Rome), "The kings of the earth who committed fornication
with her and wallowed in her sensuality will weep and lament over
her when they see the smoke arise as she burns."

However, in Chapter 17, Verses 16 and 17, of Revelation, St. John
tells us that the kings of the earth will turn on the harlot and destroy
her "and set her on fire."

Two events and two separate entities are being described, therefore. One, the city Rome, and two, mystery Babylon—the false religious system.

The harlot, as you may well realize, is used throughout the Old
Testament and the New Testament to signify a religion which prostitutes itself. In the Old Testament the prophets quite frequently
refer to Israel as a harlot because she has sold out to pagan religious
practices and/or materialistic desires. She has sold herself as does a
prostitute, for the sake of worldly gain or to worship the false gods
of the pagans. She is involved in the persecution of the true Church
and also she is "drunk with the blood of the Saints (i.e., Jews) and
the martyrs of Jesus (i.e., Christians)" (Rev. 17:6). No wonder John
was baffled!

So, in Revelation, the harlot is the religious system, the church,
which has prostituted herself. She has sold out to Anti-Christ and
his forces, joined with the kings of this world for the sake of worldly
gains and—as it will turn out—to worship a false god, none other
than Satan himself.

I will now line up all the diverse elements we have to deal with
regarding the harlot church in step by step fashion. Personally, I
find such an approach most helpful. Perhaps you will also.

(1) The great apostasy, the "falling away," a sign preliminary to
the Rapture, included one-third of the bishops of the Church plus
many millions of people around the world.

(2) Then—as you well know by now!—the Rapture took place.
All members of the Mystical Body of Christ in the state of sanctifying grace were removed from danger, taken from this world and the
time of the great tribulation to be with Our Lord.

(3) All the people left upon this earth after the Rapture are those
who either are members of the Mystical Body of Christ *not* in the
state of sanctifying grace or are those who knowingly and deliberately have disassociated themselves from the true Church.

(4) Now, at the moment of the Rapture a newly elected Pope is
raptured. In the confusion that results the forces of Anti-Christ
within and without the Vatican seize control of the election pro-
ceedings.

(5) Those members of the college of cardinals who have not been raptured for one reason or another but who, nevertheless, hold fast to their received faith hastily elect another Pope and this Pope, a true Pope, flees Rome together with them.

(6) Those members of the college of cardinals who are allies of Anti-Christ elect a pope, the Anti-Pope, and he seizes control of Vatican City with the aid of his colleagues and the forces of Anti-Christ.

Consider these words which Pope Paul VI addressed to those who had gathered for his weekly general audience on May 12, 1976: "Man's enemies, Jesus said, shall be those of his own house. How common and close to us this suffering is today. At times *our dearest friends, our most trusted colleagues, our brothers sitting at the same table* are those who have turned against us. Dissent has become habit, unfaithfulness an affirmation of freedom."

(7) Anti-Pope now heads the harlot church. This church includes all those who apostasized, fell away, from the True Church prior to the Rapture and includes (or will very shortly include) all members of other "Christian" churches who knowingly and willingly had cut themselves off from the True Church of Christ.

(8) We know that Anti-Pope will rule over a "one-world" religion because St. John tells us that "the waters on which you saw the harlot enthroned are large numbers of peoples and nations and tongues" (Rev. 17:15). It seems clear to me, but perhaps I should mention that a "one-world" religion will not include those of Moslem persuasion nor those who profess or belong to the religions of the East, Buddhism, Taoism, Shintoism, Hinduism, and so forth. These other religions exist mostly in areas not under Anti-Christ's direct control.

(9) The "one-world" religion will be a kind of watered down Christianity. To this end Anti-Pope, working with and for Anti-Christ, will proceed to eliminate certain traditional and specifically Catholic practices as devotion to the Eucharist, a belief in the Real Presence. This will be a step by step process occurring over a period of years (probably about seven years, from the time of the Rapture to the time of setting up the Abomination of Desolation in the Temple in Jerusalem). The Sacrifice of the Mass should devolve into a worship service, I think. Too, traditional Catholic devotion to Our Blessed Lady would have to be abolished. Anti-Pope will preach that such practices are no longer necessary, that Christ is now present physically in his glorified state. Anti-Pope will then point to Anti-Christ as the true Christ, come to dwell with all men forever. Anything in any way relating to the Real but spiritual and sacramental Presence of Our Lord in the world would have to be

destroyed. Anti-Christ is now present and every effort will be made to focus all honor, praise and glory on him, the evil one who strives to usurp and take the place of Our Lord.

(10) During the three and a half years between the Rapture and the Russian invasion of Israel members of the True Church, i.e., all members of the Mystical Body of Christ who maintain and stand firm in their faith, proclaiming Jesus as Lord, will suffer persecution and win the martyr's crown, the ultimate gift of man to God, even as it was the ultimate gift of God to man. The harlot church, joined to Anti-Christ in an unholy alliance, will be "drunk with the blood of God's holy ones and the blood of those martyred for their faith in Jesus" (Rev. 17:6).

(11) Since all honor will be paid to a man, Anti-Christ, which will in turn lead to a worship of man—a man indwelt by Satan— man must stand at the apex of all human striving, not God. Therefore an atheistic humanism, which has its roots in liberal rationalism and modernism, will be the philosophy of the day. Should we be alive during these days we will hear much of loving our neighbor, nothing of loving God. Man, mankind, will be deified.

(12) It is quite probable not only that Anti-Pope will do all in his power to focus all honor and glory upon Anti-Christ but also that Anti-Pope will exercise some authority over Anti-Christ and the ten rulers of the ten nation confederation.

(13) Anti-Christ will *start* to extend the sphere of his actual power and authority now, moving his forces, his armies toward the south, the east—and also toward the glorious land (Israel). In Daniel, Chapter 8, Verse 9, we are told that the "little horn," i.e., Anti-Christ, will grow toward the south, the east and the glorious land. Anti-Christ, then, will prepare for and set in motion those military operations necessary to a successful invasion of North African lands, Eastern European lands, the while quite possibly formulating stratagems for the take-over of Israel.

(14) We have mentioned, and it would be wise to keep in mind, that Anti-Christ's sphere of *influence* will be world-wide. He will exercise considerable influence throughout the African continent and also throughout South America. However, certain countries will not be directly involved in this world drama centered around Anti-Christ. They will suffer the world-wide tribulations, plagues, etc. But they will not be involved directly with Anti-Christ. These countries are, as listed in the Bible, "Tarshish and the young lions." At the time of the Russian invasion of Israel we are told that "Sheba and Dedan, the merchants of Tarshish and all her young lions shall

ask you: 'Is it for plunder that you have come?' " (Ezek. 38:13). It seems possible that Sheba and Dedan are districts of southeast Arabia.[1] As for "Tarshish and the young lions," we are told, in Ezekiel, Chapter 27, Verse 12, that the Phoenicians traded with the people of Tarshish for silver, iron, tin, and lead. Tin is the clue. As far as we know the one place where tin was available in these ancient times was Cornwall in Britain. It seems a logical step to assume that Tarshish is Britain, a merchant people and a maritime power whose emblem is the lion. The "young lions" would be Britain's "offspring": the United States, Canada, South Africa, Australia, New Zealand. These are nations which will be friendly towards Israel; too, they will not be part of Anti-Christ's empire or fall within the sphere of his direct influence. Many other nations are also mentioned in Scripture as being separate from Anti-Christ's power bloc.

(15) Judging by the description given by St. John at the time of her destruction (Rev. 18:11–19), Rome will be the cultural, sophisticated city of wealth, a city worthy, indeed, to be Anti-Christ's capital. Rome will be one of the world's wealthiest cities and a world center of materialistic culture. For those of us who live in the northeastern United States and remember New York City when that city was very probably the world's wealthiest city and truly a world capital, the Rome of Anti-Christ's Empire is easy to visualize.

(16) I sincerely hope you are balancing this entire listing of events with the series of events we discussed under the heading of the breaking of the seven seals. There exists an overlapping and many of these events—necessarily listed and discussed as separate entities—are all occurring during the same time span, the three and a half years between the Rapture and the Russian invasion.

Before turning to a detailed discussion of the Russian invasion, I should mention that Anti-Christ's government will be fascist in nature. This means, by definition, that individual ownership and enterprise are the basis for business and trade, but under strict central governmental control. I need not describe such a government further. I think most of us are reasonably familiar with the governments of Italy (1919–1945), of Germany (1933–1945), of Spain (1936–1976) in this our present age. It is the capitalistic system but under strict governmental control, with government officials acting in executive capacities in the world of business and trade.

(I sometimes have the uneasy feeling that here in the United

---

[1] Perhaps the area of the United Arab Emirates and Saudi Arabia.

States we have the exact opposite, an amalgam of government and business but with business and trade officials acting in executive capacities in the world of government.)

And I should point out yet another fascinating aspect of Anti-Christ's empire. Slavery will exist. Slaves will be bought and sold in the marketplace. Of course, in a certain sense nothing is new. Slavery has existed throughout the history of mankind. It exists today. And, here again, we certainly should be aware of the slave labor camps of the world wars and of the infamous Russian slave camps in Siberia, the Siberian salt mines. So, as I say, nothing is really new. If, here in the United States, in the year of Our Lord 1976, you do not know and understand and feel, in some little way at the very least, the degrading, sordid obscenity that the barter of human beings is, nothing I can say in this book will possibly bridge such a chasm.[1]

In any event, I do not say these things gratuitously. A number of Scripture texts are indicative of and support the statements I have just made. However, I'll introduce here a text which describes the fall and destruction of Rome. This we will deal with in the following chapter. In any event, to quote St. John:

" 'Alas! alas! thou great city, thou mighty city, Babylon! In one hour has thy judgment come.'

"And the merchants of the earth weep and mourn for her, since no one buys their cargo any more, cargo of gold, silver, jewels and pearls, fine linen, purple, silk and scarlet, all kinds of scented wood, all articles of ivory, all articles of costly wood, bronze, iron and marble, cinnamon, spice, incense, myrrh, frankincense, wine, oil, fine flour and wheat, cattle and sheep, horses and chariots, and *slaves, that is, human souls.*

" 'The fruit for which thy soul longed has gone from thee, and all thy dainties and thy splendor are lost to thee, never to be found again!'

"The merchants of these wares, who gained wealth from her, will stand far off, in fear of her torment, weeping and mourning aloud" (Rev. 18:10–15). RSV

The particular quotation I have given you deals, of course, with the destruction of Rome which will occur toward the end of Anti-Christ's reign. However, it highlights, very nicely, the slave trade and the trafficking in human souls which will go on throughout the

---

[1] This Ms. was finished in 1976 (Aug.). Since then Haley's book *Roots* has been widely read. This book, or the TV Special based on it, presents a vivid picture of the horrors of slavery.

ten and a half years of Anti-Christ's reign. During the first part of that reign it will be members of the True Church left behind at the time of the Rapture who will suffer, among other things, the indignity of slavery. However, toward the latter part of Anti-Christ's reign, it will be the Jews who will be sold into slavery. This will happen once the abomination of desolation is set up in the Temple.

Before dealing with the problem of slavery and other related matters we had better take a look at the events which precede them. Approximately three and a half years into Anti-Christ's reign over the earth, the sixth seal is broken by Our Lord (Rev. 6:12–17) and St. John records for us violent upheavals in nature. He tells us that there will be a violent earthquake, the sun will turn black, and the moon grow red as blood. The stars in the sky will fall crashing to earth like figs shaken loose by a mighty wind. The sky, as it were, will disappear, mountains and islands will be uprooted. Kings and commoners, free men and *slaves*, all will try to hide in the mountains, in caves, and they will cry out: "Fall on us! Hide us from the face of One who sits on the throne and from the wrath of the Lamb! The great day of their vengeance has come. Who can withstand it?"

These catastrophic events, listed at this point by St. John, correspond with the first of the signs in Joel depicting a day of darkness and of gloom. Such upheavals have occurred during recorded history,[1] and they are predicted as coming on three separate occasions in the latter days by Joel. Revelation and Matthew also refer to them. "The Day of the Lord is coming." Note that text. Some translations read: "*before* the day of the Lord." This is the proper meaning. And before the day of the Lord, the Second Coming, arrives, prior to the actual time of Our Lord's return to this earth, Israel will be invaded by an army from the north. Joel describes this invasion in frightening terms. The invaders are "like a mighty people arrayed for battle. Before them peoples are in torment, every face blanches" (Joel 2:5–6).

However, the Lord will be stirred to concern for His land and His people. Thus, He says: "No, the *northerner* I will remove far from you, and drive him out into a land arid and waste, with his van toward the eastern sea, and his rear toward the western sea; and his foulness shall go up, and his stench shall go up" (Joel 2:20).

I would ask you now to turn to the prophet Ezekiel. We must now study in some depth his 38th and 39th chapters. It is in these chapters that we find the very famous prophecies about Gog and Magog. Given in three subdivisions, each of which adds further detail, the

[1] See Velikovsky, *Ages in Chaos*, Doubleday, N.Y., 1952.

prophecy speaks out against, inveighs against a foreign leader, Gog, from a foreign land, Magog, who invades Israel. This invasion of Israel by Russia is the invasion of the northern enemy as prophesied by Joel which prophecy corresponds, time-wise, to the breaking of the sixth seal in St. John.

Now, let's take a closer look at Ezekiel. Gog and Magog refer to Russia. Translations vary a bit, of course. The opening lines of Ezekiel's 38th chapter are translated, in the New American Bible, as:

"Thus the word of the Lord came to me: Son of man, turn toward Gog (the land of Magog), the chief prince of Meshech and Tubal, and prophesy against him."

Another translation, the rendering of the Jerusalem Bible, reads:

"The word of Yahweh was addressed to me as follows, Son of man, turn toward Gog and the country of Magog, the prince of Rosh, Meshech, and Tubal, and prophesy against him."

The second translation is a more accurate rendering of the Hebrew text. In either case Russia is meant. While the meaning of the words "Gog" and "Magog" is uncertain, it is known that Meshech and Tubal were lands around the Black Sea, lands which are now part of Russia. Too, it has been ascertained that Rosh was an ancient name for today's Russia. "USSR Russian Federation" (Novasti Press Agency, Moscow, p. 12) states:

"In the 6th century A.D. different tribes began to form alliances, headed by the most powerful *princes*. It was thus that the first state associations arose among the East Slavs. The centre of one of these unions was the tribe of *Ros* or *Rus*. The name of this tribe was later extended to all the East Slavs who began to be called Russians and the territory in which they lived, Russian land or Rus."

Without question the northern enemy is Russia and at some future date it will attack and invade Israel. Please read, now, Ezekiel, Chapter 38, Verses 4 to 6. "I will lead you forth with all your army, horses and riders all handsomely outfitted, a great horde with bucklers and shields, all of them carrying swords: Persia, Cush and Put with them (all with shields and helmets), Gomer with all its troops, Beth-togar-mah FROM THE RECESSES OF THE NORTH with all its troops, many people with you."

This is the horde, the peoples, nations who will comprise the invading force which will overrun Israel. Please make a special note that this force and this leader are from the FAR NORTH. Ezekiel refers to this fact three times. Moscow, by the way, happens to be directly north of Jerusalem, on the same longitude. This is most important since Anti-Christ is referred to as the king of the north in Daniel and we will be dealing with that problem very shortly. At this point in time however, in recounting the chronology of Anti-Christ's kingdom, we are treating of a leader, a prince, Gog, from the *far* north.

It just occurred to me that if you went any further north of Israel than Russia you would be at the North Pole amongst a few Eskimos, who are, I am reasonably sure, not about to invade Israel. No, it is Russia, who is uncommonly interested in the Near East and in Africa, that we have to watch.

I will list for you a few of the details of this Russian invasion, as described in the 38th and 39th chapters of Ezekiel:

(1) At the time of the invasion the Israelites will be living in security. [Also, since other nations of the world will have been impoverished by the four horsemen of the apocalypse, Israel will be quite wealthy, at least relatively speaking (Ezek. 28:13).] They will be living in villages or towns without walls or gates and they will be at peace. Remember Anti-Christ brought about "peace and security."

(2) The Russian army and its allies will descend upon Israel suddenly and plunder and pillage the open villages and towns.

(3) The merchants of Tarshish (Great Britain) and all her young lions (as we have already seen, the United States, Canada, South Africa, Australia, New Zealand—the offspring, that is, those countries and/or territories once the colonies of Britain) will protest. This will be in the nature of a diplomatic protest since there is no mention of military intervention. [Tarshish will have a naval base at Tyre (Isaiah 23:1–38). It will be destroyed (Isaiah 23:14), perhaps now, or possibly in the later war. When this base is built, the identification of Tarshish will become more certain.]

No mention is made of Anti-Christ or his empire. I would, therefore, assume that there will be no military intervention by Anti-Christ at this point, either. It may well be the Russian invasion will be triggered by the military activities of Anti-Christ, the spread of his kingdom. Perhaps the political and military maneuverings of Anti-Christ pose a threat or appear threatening to Russia, or to Russian interests in the Near East. (Recall, if you will, the invasions of Russia by Napoleon and by Hitler.) In any event, whatever the cause, the invasion occurs.

Then, again to use a favorite phrase in describing these last years of this present age, all hell breaks loose. The Lord God will:

(1) Cause a great shaking upon the land of Israel.

(2) All living creatures will tremble before the wrath of God.

(3) Mountains shall be overturned, cliffs shall tumble, walls shall fall to the ground.

(4) Pestilence, bloodshed, flooding rain and hailstones, fire and brimstone will be unleashed against the northern enemy.

(5) Moreover, the Lord God will slay all the troops of the Russians.

(6) The birds of the air and the wild beasts will feed upon the slain troops.

(7) Furthermore, the Lord God will send fire upon Russia and also those who live in the coastlands that "they shall know that I am the Lord" (Ezek. 38:18-23).

To have all these catastrophes occurring simultaneously cannot be explained naturally. In a word, Russia will be clobbered and this will be clearly the Lord's doing!

Ezekiel does not hesitate to describe the gory aftermath of this holocaust. Firstly, the inhabitants of Israel will be able to use the weapons of war captured from or abandoned by the Russians as fuel for SEVEN years. Prior to the invasion they had been cutting wood from the forests for fuel. (Why they should have to be cutting wood in the forests for fuel is an intriguing question. In any case, Palestine had been almost bare of trees for centuries. The 100,000,000 trees planted during the last 30 years are now almost ready for cutting.) Now, to have enough fuel to last for *seven years* seems impossible, in light of conventional warfare and, also in light of the type of attack the Russians will launch against Israel. The descriptions seem to call for a kind of blitzkrieg, especially an invasion by air with paratroopers invading and attacking all over the place. However, in light of modern atomic warfare, a seven years' supply of fuel is suddenly very, very possible. The component parts of one or two or several atomic bombs might well be the booty of this particular war and could be used to fuel nuclear reactors.

Secondly, Gog will be buried in the Valley of Abarim, along with all his horde. Men will be employed to go about the land burying the dead. This shall continue over a period of seven months. The birds of the air, the wild beasts will feed on the flesh of soldiers, of horses; they will drink the blood of these soldiers, warriors, horses. During these days, when the sun sets, the quiet of the evening will be disturbed only by the rustling of a feather and the occasional gentle belch of a vulture.

The picture is a bloody one. To visualize the scene, bring to mind the pictures of the horrible atrocities of the Vietnam war in which we were but recently engaged. I think all of us have seen more than enough of such scenes either in the newspapers or in the TV news programs. Transpose all those scenes to the Mid-East and you have the picture. The soldiers parachuting into Israel and also attacking with land forces; the looting, burning, killing, raping. Success seems inevitable. Anti-Christ makes no move to stop the carnage; nor does the United States. The best the United States can do is offer a diplomatic protest.

THEN—the wrath of God descends upon the Russian army and destroys it. Earthquakes, volcanic eruptions, violent atmospheric disturbances. Thence, dead soldiers, mutilated bodies strewn about, blood staining the earth, vultures swooping down to gorge themselves on human flesh, wolves, bears, the large cats, the wild carnivorous beasts of the area tearing at the flesh of the legs and arms, torsos of freshly killed human beings. (Scenes from Alfred Hitchcock's *The Birds* come to mind.) I am not being melodramatic. I do want you to visualize the scene in all its reality, a bloody, ghastly mess.

The Divine Purpose for all this activity, this devastating defeat of the Russian army, is to turn the Israelites from their merely natural and materialistic concept of life, from their almost purely worldly views and desires with regard to the Promised Land. This Russian debacle will cause the conversion of at least some Israelites *to God*. Such utter destruction will also make an impact upon the other nations of the world. Now many people around the world will turn to God. Of course, the Russians invade Israel only. However, the *effects* of God's wrath are seen and experienced around the world (Ezek. 39:6; 39:21). Small wonder then that some people, at least, come to their senses and turn to God. I am more amazed by the fact that many people will persist in their sin. Despite everything that has thus far occurred all over the world people will persist in leading sinful lives. Astonishing, really. It has been suggested that, at this time, Russia will be converted, thus fulfilling one of the prophecies of private revelation at Fatima. This, I would think, is a very good possibility.

I should hasten to point out that such conversions as do occur in Israel are conversions to God, not to Our Lord. Many Jewish people will return to a faith in God, but they will not yet turn to Our Lord. St. John, however, in Chapter 14 of Revelation, does mention 144,000 of the twelve tribes of Israel who are sealed with the sign of the Lamb and His Father on their foreheads. The one hundred and forty-four thousand of Chapter 7 and the one hundred and forty-four thousand men "who have never been defiled by immorality with women" of Chapter 14 of Revelation are, apparently, one and

the same group of men. They are with Our Lord as He stands upon
Mount Zion at the time of the Second Coming. This group of men
(sorry about that, Women's Lib!) are quite special. They are sealed
with the mark of the Lamb. Thus they are protected during the time
of persecution, the Jewish persecution, at least from death. Apparently they are to remain here (in Israel, that is) to greet Our Lord
at His Second Coming, since they have been ransomed as the first
fruits of mankind for God and the slain Lamb.

In any event, this group of virgin Jewish men is converted to Our
Lord. One hundred forty-four thousand is a small number, compared to the number of priests and male religious in the Church
right now. Perhaps virginity, which has been the pride and glory of
the priesthood and religious life for centuries will have gone out of
style and repute then, when the true Church is underground so that
even this small number attracts attention. Perhaps it is because
they are Jews, and the concept of virginity will be an innovation for
the Jews then. Either way, virginity is a special virtue, and these
144,000 are singled out for a special reward in the future life. Virginity (or chastity) after all is the exclusiveness of love, reserving
oneself for one's future spouse. It is similar to married fidelity,
reserving oneself for one's present spouse. These are virgins who
have reserved themselves for God as an expression of their love for
God. After the wedding feast of the Lamb they get their reward.
Needless to say virginity does not rule out the practice of other
virtues, but rather presupposes them. Here their truthfulness is
singled out also. They did not deny their belief in God, during a
time of persecution. "They are pure and follow the Lamb wherever
he goes . . . On their lips no deceit has been found, they are indeed without flaw" (Rev. 14:4–5). But this is not true for most of the
Jewish community. Many of the ordinary people will turn to God.
The Israeli government, which could well be a minority government, of course, however, now enters into a "firm covenant" with
Anti-Christ. As Daniel says: For one "week" (i.e., seven years) he
(i.e., Anti-Christ) will make a firm compact with the many (i.e., the
faithless Jews who ally themselves with Anti-Christ rather than
with God) (Dan. 9:27). This seems to be the covenant referred to in
Dan. 11:22; Isaiah 28:15–18 describes this vividly as a "covenant
with death!"

Of course, on a purely natural level I can understand why the
Israeli government would do this. They are and will be a small
beleaguered land between the powerful empire of Anti-Christ to
the north and the reasonably powerful forces of Egypt to the south.
Israel had not been protected by "Tarshish" (i.e., England, possi-

bly) or the United States; anyway both of these may have been among the distant coastlands that had fire rained on them, leaving Israel pretty much alone. [Tarshish's ships, however, will be available after Armageddon to return all Jewish people to the Land of the Promise (Isaiah 60:9).] The Israeli government will turn to Anti-Christ for protection. And therein we have the final tragedy. God's chosen people turn to God's most bitter enemy, Satan, for protection. And right after their miraculous delivery from Russia, too!

We must next consider the seven plagues God will now unleash upon the earth to try to bring all peoples to their senses and to turn to Him willingly and freely. (Israel's treaty with Anti-Christ runs for seven years, Israel's fuel supply lasts for seven years, and seven plagues are coming. Fascinating!) The seal judgments corresponded to natural catastrophes, quite often. Men refused to see in these judgments the finger of God. Very well, then, God will now visit judgments upon mankind which are a definite sign of His wrath. Men will know for certain that the seven plagues symbolized by trumpets and bowls in St. John's Revelation are of Divine origin.

During this time the Spirit will be poured out upon all mankind. Persecution against those true believers and Church members yet alive will now cease. Anti-Christ's three and a half year period for this activity is up. The *True* Church, as a visible organization, apparently no longer exists. True Church members now cannot look to a visible Church truly of Christ for guidance. Thus they will have the guidance of the Holy Spirit directly since an *effective* true Church organization no longer exists. Our Lord did say: "I am with you always, until the end of the world!" (Mt. 16:19). But Mother Church is underground, persecuted. This outpouring of the Spirit will begin after the time of the Russian invasion and continue until the time of the Second Coming, that is, for seven years. The prophet Joel speaks of this outpouring of the Spirit:

Then afterward I will pour out my spirit upon all mankind. Your sons and daughters shall prophesy, Your old men shall dream dreams, Your young men shall see visions; Even upon the servants and the handmaids, in those days, I will pour out my spirit. (Joel 3:1–2)

This prophecy was partially fulfilled at the time of Pentecost (Acts 2:14–21). The phrases "upon *all* mankind" and "in those days" indicate quite clearly that the prophecy awaits complete fulfillment. This will happen following upon the Russian debacle and during the time of the seven final plagues, the trumpet/bowl judgments.

As always God grants to all of us His grace, His very life. We have but to respond. The old adage is ever true: we must pray as if everything depended on God; we must work as if everything depended on us. By faith and good works we will save our souls, but, should we be alive during the final seven years of Anti-Christ's reign we will share in that great outpouring of the Spirit. We may be living in some refuge, a hidden cave, a cellar, an attic; we may be in concentration camps. Still the Spirit will be ours that we may follow the Lamb when He returns to us.

But we should understand that we possess the Spirit now, this very minute. We should know that God is with us and in us now, at this very moment. God, Father, Son, and Holy Spirit, dwell with us, in us that we—God and you, God and me—may be as one at the marriage feast of the Lamb.

VII
Armageddon

Part I
The Abomination of Desolation

In the previous chapter we took a look at Anti-Christ and the development of his empire during the first three and a half years of his reign. We also considered the Anti-Pope and the development of the harlot church. Finally we studied, in some detail, the Russian invasion of Israel.

We have now to consider the final seven years of Anti-Christ's reign, seven years which will culminate in the great war of Armageddon.

To begin. In St. John's book of Revelation, Chapter 8, the scene is set for the second great portent, the second warning to all men that they should repent of their sins, turn to God and call upon His mercy. The scene is easy to visualize, at least for those familiar with the new rite of the Roman Catholic Mass. As St. John describes this heavenly scene, you look toward a throne (God's throne) and before that throne you see the golden altar upon which rest the prayers of the saints. An angel stands at the altar with a golden censer and the incense from the censer mingles with the prayers of the saints. I do not think that those responsible for the revision and restructuring of the Mass had any intention of mimicking this scene. However, this would describe quite accurately the sanctuaries of most Catholic churches today. As you look toward the sanctuary from the body (or nave) of the church, you see a throne (here in the United States we call it a President's chair) before which stands the altar of Sacrifice (which is tautological since an altar is simply the place where sacrifice is offered). During the celebration of the liturgy you can see, around that altar, the chief celebrant, perhaps several other priests, altar-boys, lectors, extraordinary ministers. You will even see a

117

censer being used in its proper place, incense pouring forth to mingle with the prayers of the faithful upon the altar.

Given the scene, the heavenly sanctuary, a number of extraordinary things now begin to occur. First, however, for some unknown reason there is silence in heaven, for about half an hour. No one knows what this means so it is senseless to waste any time guessing at its meaning. Perhaps it simply represents a definitive break from past events and the beginning of the new events, the five plagues to be unleashed upon sinful mankind, God's second warning that the end is imminent. This should serve to indicate that God is most displeased with us and to give us fair warning that Our Lord is about to come again upon this earth, now in power and glory. In all this, God's purpose always is: to try to bring men to their senses and to turn them to the true God, their Lord and Creator.

The blowing of a trumpet, the pouring out of the contents of a bowl or vial: these symbols indicate the beginning of each plague. Thus, when the first trumpet blows, hail and fire mixed with blood fall upon the earth. A third of the earth is burnt up, a third of the trees is burnt up, and all the green grass is burnt up.

Now, if you are reading along in your New Testament about these horrendous calamities, you will readily realize that the "trumpet and bowl" scenes describe the same series of events (Revs. 8 and 9; Rev. 16). The descriptive details may vary a bit, but the central occurrence or episode is, essentially, the same. This is in keeping with the command St. John receives "to prophesy *again* about many peoples and nations and tongues and kings" (Rev. 10:11). He has already recorded the "trumpet prophecies." Now he must record these prophecies over again. This he does in the "bowl prophecies." He tells us that men who are branded with the mark of the beast and worship the image of the beast will be afflicted with foul and evil sores.

Let us now strive to pull all these disparate facts together. AntiChrist's empire especially will be the object of God's wrath. However, all mankind is afflicted by these plagues. Looking now just at the first plague, it is clear that great areas of Europe will become dust bowls. This will be true, however, also in the United States, in South and Central America, in Africa, in China—all over the world. John Steinbeck's *The Grapes of Wrath* serves as a fine example. Just take some of the dust bowl scenes depicted in that novel and movie, scenes of our own west and southwest in the thirties, and transpose these scenes, in your imagination, to one-third of the United States—indeed, one-third of each of the countries in the world—and you've got it: the first plague. A disturbing picture, to say the least. At the same time those people who have received the mark of the beast will be afflicted with pus-filled, foul-smelling, evil-looking sores all over their bodies. I would assume that a great many of these disease-ridden people will be living within the boundaries of Anti-Christ's empire. However, this affliction (the description of which brings to mind the secondary stages of syphilis) will certainly not be confined just to Anti-Christ's empire. It will affect people all over the world, all those who have received the mark of the beast (i.e., Anti-Christ).

Now, you may be sure that Anti-Christ will move to do all in his power to counter these Divinely instigated disasters now occurring within and without his empire. It is, therefore, quite likely that Anti-Christ will seek to extend his empire, in one way or another, thus de-emphasizing domestic problems by emphasizing foreign affairs, a classic pattern.

So—to put it as bluntly as I can, we are now involved in a kind of juggling act. In these final seven years of Anti-Christ's reign so many things occur, and often at the same time, that we must be like a juggler keeping five or six or even seven balls up in the air and in active play all at the same time. As long as you understand that a number of events are going on, many at the same time and extending over several years, then the picture—a constantly shifting, kaleidoscopic, rapidly moving picture—is getting through to you.

But to continue. The second trumpet is blown and apparently some sort of planetoid strikes the earth, plunging into the sea. This catastrophic event causes the sea to become as blood, destroys one-third of the world's shipping and causes the destruction of one-third of all marine life. The description, here, is most probably, of all the oceans of the world. The spilling, or outpouring, of the second bowl depicts a similar scene. The details vary only slightly. The sea is described as becoming like the blood of a dead man and everything dies that is in the sea. As you can see, some detail is added. Also, the description here is, in all probability, of the Mediterranean Sea only. As some authors have noted, there is really little or no difference between the trumpets and the bowls save for the viewpoint. From a heavenly viewpoint it would seem as if the plagues occur at the sound of the trumpet, formally announced, as it were. From an earthly point of view it seems as if the plagues are poured out upon the earth as if from a bowl.

Now, while I am thinking about it, I must interject two other thoughts. A progressive order exists with regard to these seven plagues (or blows, stripes, those things which smite or trouble,

harass or torment; an evil scourge), the final sign to mankind prior
to the actual moment of the Second Coming. Note the progression:

1st trumpet-bowl	the earth	Rev. 8:7	Rev. 16:2
2nd trumpet-bowl	the sea	Rev. 8:8	Rev. 16:3
3rd trumpet-bowl	the rivers	Rev. 8:10	Rev. 16:4–7
4th trumpet-bowl	the sun	Rev. 8:12	Rev. 16:8–9
5th trumpet-bowl	the seat of Anti-Christ	Rev. 9:1–11	Rev. 16:10–11
6th trumpet-bowl	the river Euphrates	Rev. 9:12–21	Rev. 16:12–16
7th trumpet-bowl	the return of Our Lord	Rev. 11:15–19	Rev. 16:17–20

What is involved in this progression of plagues is the disruption
and destruction of the elements essential to our very life, our
natural life, that is. A quick glance at that list should alert us to the
fact that shortly, perhaps in our own lifetime, the ecology is about
to be badly messed up. That delicate balance so desirable and
necessary in nature is about to be thrown badly out of whack.

My second thought: the striking use of symbolism. When Joshua
fought the battle of Jericho the walls fell down. True. But the manner of conquest fascinates. The city was taken by trumpets. On the
seventh day of the attack the Israelites marched around the city
walls and blew their trumpets. The seventh time around the trumpets were blown, the walls fell down and the city was made captive.

In the same manner, when God prepares to wrest the earth from
Satan's grasp, seven seals are broken. Then seven trumpets are
sounded, one at a time. At the sounding of the seventh trumpet, the
cities of the world fall and God's kingdom is established upon
earth.

But to return to a consideration of the scenes of the trumpets and
bowls. Just think about the underlying meaning of the words in the
second trumpet-bowl. A third part of all marine life destroyed! A
major source of our food supplies is destroyed. As a result malnutri-
tion and starvation will be widespread. Think of the great numbers
of ships destroyed, the men of the Merchant Marine, the Navy
slain. This will be another Pearl Harbor, only many, many times
worse. Have any of you seen the movie *The Poseidon Adventure?*
The people—men, women, children—screaming, struggling to escape as that great ship capsizes and plunges to the bottom. Or bring
to mind the pictures made of the sinking of the *Titanic.* Magnify
each of these disasters a thousand times over and you just begin to
grasp the enormity and horror of the second plague.

As for the third plague, we are told that at the sounding of the trumpet a great star falls from the heavens. Since it is described as burning like a lamp, it may be that a meteor will be the instrument to achieve the effects of this plague. This burning star, given the name Wormwood, falls upon the third part of the rivers and upon the fountains of waters. It so contaminates a third of the world's water supply that the waters of the world become like wormwood, that is, bitter, causing the death of many men.

You quite probably realize that wormwood is a bitter herb. It is a cultivated herb, growing in herb gardens where you can see and taste it. For example if you live near the Morristown National Park in New Jersey, as I do, you can visit the Herb garden of the Tempe Wick House and see and, perhaps, taste this extremely acrid herb for yourself. That is how one-third of the world's water supply will taste, so bitter as even to cause death. Many areas of the earth will have people crying out, as did the ancient mariner: water, water, everywhere, and not a drop to drink.

I remind you, once again, the damage inflicted by this plague, and the others as well, will occur in Anti-Christ's empire. However, the effects will also be felt worldwide. If we are alive at the time here in the United States, we will suffer from the plagues too. Very few people will escape. Perhaps people living in Australia or New Zealand, maybe, will not be so badly affected. But even in these far distant places the effects of the plagues will be experienced.

The further detail of this third plague is that the rivers and fountains of waters will become as blood. That description puts me in mind of a time in my life when I lived in lower Jersey City. Perhaps the water is better now but at the time water drawn from the faucet was a rusty red—thickened with a kind of red sediment. The water was completely undrinkable as it came from the tap. So the condition of an undrinkable bloody water supply is an easy one for me to imagine.

Too, I am sure we have all heard of the terrible sufferings of the survivors of shipwrecks (ships torpedoed during the war, for example). These persons would have to endure the intense heat of the sea by day, the intense cold of the sea by night, and surrounded by water—salt water, they were unable to slake their burning thirst. Those who were no longer able to endure their thirst gulped down the salt water—and died.

From all this you should be able to imagine the horrible thirst you may have to endure should you be alive at the time of this plague. If you can't, just do this. The next time you are thirsty and you are about to drink a glass of water—stop. Put off drinking that water you really want for three or four hours. You will shortly experience what it is like to be without water.

Having spilled the blood of the saints and the prophets men are now punished, in turn, by having their water supply become as blood (Rev. 16:6).

As these plagues continue, attacking Anti-Christ and his empire, hopefully people will turn from their evil ways, from Satan to God. Despite the serious difficulties he is experiencing, Anti-Christ is actively campaigning to expand the actual physical area of his empire and to extend his influence all over the world. Small wars, invasions, military conquests will be the order of the day, as well as diplomatic ruses, ploys, skirmishes, maneuvers. The plagues continue to decimate the people of the world, especially the people of Anti-Christ's empire, including all those in the armed forces of that empire. Russia is recuperating from the devastating blow which well-nigh destroyed her as a world power. But she is starting to regain her strength. Egypt continues to build up her military power.

Anti-Christ—still playing the role of Israel's protector—allows worship and the offering of sacrifices in the Temple at Jerusalem. That Temple may well be rebuilt by this time. It may not be completely finished but it is probably near completion, at least, since worship and animal sacrifices will have been restored in the Temple by this time. We can know this because Anti-Christ will abolish sacrifice and oblation in the Temple about three and a half years before his reign over the earth comes to an end. Since Anti-Christ halts sacrifice and oblation, sacrifice and oblation must be a present reality. Since Anti-Christ halts sacrifice and oblation in the Temple, it follows that the Temple must be a present reality (Dan. 9:27).

Rome, too, the center of Anti-Christ's empire, has become and will remain—for a few more years—the great city of culture and sophistication (Rev. 18:14–17; 21–24), but also the sin city of the world, Babylon, as St. John labels Rome.

Keep in mind, also, the continuing activities of the harlot church and Anti-Pope. Even as God is sending these plagues upon men to try to bring them to Himself, the harlot church, headed by Anti-Pope, is doing all in her power to win men over to honor and serve Anti-Christ. This is truly the false church, turning people from God to Satan!

I had best remind you, again, that these plagues will not harm or kill those who are true believers and followers of Our Lord. If we are alive at this time we will be hiding out somewhere or maybe be in concentration camps. Or maybe we'll be slaves. But we will bear the mark of the Slain Lamb on our foreheads (I would hope!). (Ezek. 9:4 is a type of the mark of the Lamb. *See also* Rev. 9:4; Rev. 22:4–5.) We will not be harmed by the plagues. Only those people who turn their backs on Our Lord, who persist in their sinful ways, who are *not* marked with the sign of the Lamb will be afflicted. "The man who holds out to the end, however, is the one who will see salvation" (Mt. 24:13).

"All will hate you because of me, yet not a hair of your heads will be harmed. By patient endurance you will save your lives" (Lk. 21:17–19).

The fourth plague now occurs. The sun, the moon, and the stars are darkened. As St. John puts it, a third part of the sun, a third part of the moon and a third part of the stars are darkened. Some sort of cataclysmic event now occurs. The earth will be cast into darkness, perhaps as happens when an eclipse of the sun or of the moon occurs. Anyone driving into New York City, for example, can observe, from a distance of thirty or forty miles, the heavy shroud of smog which hovers over the city and frequently obliterates the famous New York City skyline. I can recall being in the city one day, at about noontime, when a temperature inversion occurred. The streets became dark, a heavy stifling kind of dense yellowish fog seemed to cover the area making it difficult to breathe, streetlights went on, cars put on their headlights, and people seemed like phantoms. Yet it was twelve o'clock, noontime. I had the feeling that doomsday was upon us, a frightened feeling. I suppose a Londoner, accustomed to the famed London fog, might not have experienced the same emotions. But enough people in New York City must have experienced the same frightened feeling because the incident made the front pages of the papers the next day (which is why I know the event was caused by temperature inversion).

Perhaps the incident will help you to visualize the fourth plague. A further detail of this fourth plague is that the intense heat of the sun will cause men to think they are being scorched with fire. But even as men are being scorched with unbearable heat they still blaspheme the name of God and refuse to render proper glory to Him. This may seem astonishing to you but that is what is going to happen.

Of course, an eclipse of the sun or the moon no longer frightens us as it did our ancestors. Yet any change in the normal ordering of the sun, moon, or stars can upset us and even cause fear. Whoever it was who directed the film about Our Lady of Fatima caught that reaction of fear and trembling in the scene, one of the final scenes of that movie, when the sun seemed to dance in the sky and then

hurtle toward the earth. Many of the spectators cringed and even
fled in terror. So it will be with the fourth plague.

And I need not describe the effects of scorching heat. Anyone
who has ever spent a summer at the Jersey shore or in Florida and
has experienced the unremitting heat of the day from about one
o'clock in the afternoon until about five o'clock knows the effects of
scorching heat. Those of you who live in or have traveled through
our own Southwest are surely familiar with the heat of the desert,
and the stories of Death Valley have become a part of our heritage.
By the time of the fourth plague great areas of the earth will be just
like Death Valley in the days of the pioneers. There will be great
suffering—the due punishment of God. Yet men will still not turn
to God. Astonishing!

The first four plagues will be directed at all men wherever they
may be living on this earth. And all men, women, children will be
affected. The only people who will not be harmed are those faithful
to Our Lord. Following upon these four plagues are three final
plagues which are directed more especially at the kingdom of
Anti-Christ. God's wrath, so it would seem, is now concentrated, as
it were, focused most particularly on the empire of the beast. Because each one of these plagues will be so terrible each will also be
known as a Woe. The three woes announced by the angel in Revelation, Chapter 8, are the final three plagues prior to Our Lord's
return.

The fifth plague now occurs. The fifth trumpet sounds and a
fallen star—most probably Satan—is given the key to the bottomless pit. Obviously, all the powers of darkness and evil are about to
be unleashed against mankind. Men have pledged allegiance to
Satan. Very well. Now God will allow them to suffer the real
ministrations of the Devil. Let them see what hell is really like!

From this bottomless pit there issues a heavy black smoke which
darkens the sun and the air. For those of us who live in great
industrial centers of our country that is not difficult to visualize.
However, this fifth plague also includes an invasion of locusts who
attack humans. This is somewhat more difficult to imagine—save in
the pages of science fiction. St. John, I can assure you, was not
writing a book of science fiction. He was writing down the visions
of the end-times, granted to him by God. Precisely what he was
trying to describe remains difficult to fathom on a number of occasions. This is one.

What, precisely, is this invasion of locusts? They will have the
power of scorpions. They will torture men with their sting which is
like the sting of the scorpion. They will thus torment men for five

months. However, they will not be allowed to harm any green growth or grass or any tree but only men who do not have the seal of God upon their foreheads.

All of this upsets the normal order in nature. Of locusts we have all heard. Usually locusts attack foliage, not humans. But now they do attack humans and are prevented from destroying their natural food. Also St. John describes these creatures (or whatever it is they are) as looking like horses arrayed for battle, on their heads what looks like crowns of gold, their faces look like human faces, their hair like women's hair, their teeth like lion's teeth. They have scales like iron breastplates, the noise of their wings like the noise of many chariots with horses rushing into battle. It is interesting to note that while these beings or creatures or things have teeth like lion's teeth, the power to harm humans lies in their tails. They are able to obey commands and have as their leader the angel of the bottomless pit, Abaddon by name, which means destroyer.

The fifth bowl (which is the same as the fifth trumpet) adds that men gnaw their tongues in anguish and curse God because of their pain *and their sores*. These sores are the result of an earlier plague, the first plague. Much of the world's population will be a mangy, scrofulous looking lot, apparently. Yet, they do not repent of their sins.

We may never have seen a locust or a scorpion but we have seen pictures of them and read of them. According to what I have read the sting of the scorpion is the most painful sting a man can suffer. Just intensify, say a hundred-fold, the painful effect of a bee sting, for example. That might give you an idea of the pain and torment men will suffer during this plague. Or I can recall hiking one time to the very southern tip of Long Beach Island in New Jersey with a friend. This is a low-lying and swampy area, of course. We decided—foolishly—to return by going straight through this marshy area rather than along the ocean's edge. We were soon literally covered by a thick cloud of mosquitoes which attacked us so viciously that we actually ran out to the very edge of the ocean to escape them. Or, again, those of you who have summered at the Jersey coast are familiar, I would think, with the bite of the horsefly, a very large black fly with a vicious bite. I can recall occasions when attacking swarms of these flies actually forced people to leave the beach.

I realize these insect attacks are no longer common because of the constant use of insecticides. But readers on the older side of thirty will surely know what I'm talking about. As I have tried to describe the pain human beings can experience when attacked by

stinging creatures, so St. John tried to give expression to the torment and pain that will be inflicted upon men during the fifth
plague. Should we have to endure it, it will be a most painful
excruciating experience.

At this point—about five years prior to the actual moment of Our
Lord's Second Coming—Anti-Christ decides to attack Egypt. Considering the internal disruption the five plagues have been and are
causing within his empire, this seems an incredible thing. Yet
leaders often enough do exactly this—an external diversion from
internal difficulties. Whatever the reason, Anti-Christ mounts an
invasion of Egypt (the King of the South) and attacks that country
with a great army. This is described by Daniel in Chapter eleven of
his book. The timing of and precise nature of the events described
in verses one through twenty remain, at best, uncertain. Starting
with verse twenty-one of that eleventh chapter we are certainly
given a description of the latter days and "the contemptible person," that is, Anti-Christ, the one who comes without warning.
Verses twenty-two through twenty-four give us a synopsis of the
spread of Anti-Christ's empire. In verse twenty-five we get details
of Anti-Christ's sweep against Egypt. In turn Egypt will retaliate,
seek to defend herself with an exceedingly great and mighty army.
Reading the daily newspaper headlines, I would think that we are
now watching the preparations for this war taking place.

This time around, Egypt will be defeated, apparently cut
down—at least in part—by the plotting, the deceit of traitors within
her midst, a fifth column, as this was called during World War II.
(Actually the term "fifth column" was first used in the Spanish Civil
War. During the siege of Madrid, 1936, Franco had four columns
advancing on it, traitors in the city were the fifth column.) Having
defeated Egypt, Anti-Christ, it seems, turns toward Israel possibly
with the intention of occupying the glorious land. He is dissuaded
from doing this, apparently, by Israeli leaders. He then returns to
his own capital, Rome, with much plunder and loot. However, it is
now reasonably clear that Anti-Christ's plans do not include the
honoring of the seven-year treaty he has with Israel. His mind is set
against the holy covenant (i.e., the worship of God in the Temple at
Jerusalem). This military activity will take place, approximately,
from five to about three and a half years prior to Our Lord's Second
Coming.

Anti-Christ, so it appears, has returned to his capital, Rome.
Flushed with success, with military victory abroad, he now extends
his powers at home. He turns on the harlot church. It may well be
that the plagues which have been afflicting many millions of
people, most especially the citizens of Anti-Christ's empire, may

have actually moved some people to turn to the harlot church seeking some sort of, any sort of solace. This would represent a threat to Anti-Christ's desire for absolute power; too, the harlot church may have—indeed, probably will have—acquired possessions of great material value, great wealth. Political power, and the wherewithal to exercise that power, namely money, is threatening and tempting to any incumbent dictatorial ruler. Therefore, Anti-Christ and his cohorts, the ten rulers of the Confederation, will turn on this harlot church and strip her naked, leave her desolate and finally utterly destroy her. Much the same scenario occurred in England during the reign of Henry VIII. In England, of course, it was the True Church which was stripped and left desolate.

The buildings, the properties of the harlot church will be confiscated and harlot church leaders will be done away with, I am quite sure. However, it is more than a little interesting to note that Anti-Pope survives. Vatican City will no longer be a separate political entity ruled over by Anti-Pope. It may still *appear* to be the headquarters of the false one-world religion but now Anti-Christ and his cohorts, aided and abetted by Anti-Pope, will take full and absolute control. What will be left of the Vatican at this point I cannot say, but Anti-Pope himself will survive. He will survive because he is also a political leader. We noted, at least in passing, that he probably holds an office in Anti-Christ's kingdom, a job akin to that of secretary of the treasury.

Indeed, so perverse is Anti-Pope that he has an image of Anti-Christ made and has the people of the world worship this statue. Of course, such perverse activity is a prime reason, if not *the* prime reason, that Anti-Pope will be able to maintain his power and position in Anti-Christ's empire despite the downfall of the harlot church.

What will be happening, about three and a half years prior to the Second Coming, has happened before. As every schoolboy knows, the Roman emperors were worshipped even as Anti-Christ will be worshipped. Roman citizens and all those who wished to be considered loyal to Rome had to worship before a statue of the reigning Roman emperor and burn incense in his honor. In the end-times Anti-Pope will establish some sort of worship service to be offered before the statue of Anti-Christ. Probably Anti-Pope, through his agents, will set up shrines throughout the empire to which people will go—i.e., will *have* to go—to offer worship to Anti-Christ. I would think that the statues of Anti-Christ set up throughout the empire will be copies of the original image or statue of Anti-Christ of which St. John speaks (Rev. 13:11–15).

As St. John relates his vision, Anti-Pope is allowed to give breath to the image of Anti-Christ so that this image appears to live and is even able to speak. A speaking statue! Does that sound strange to you? It does not sound strange to me—any longer. Of late I have come across some information, something you may not yet know. I have been told by a friend—a computer expert—that computer science has now reached the stage where you will soon be able to actually speak to the computer and the computer will answer you! I know, as do you, that as of now you feed questions to a computer by typing out those questions on its keyboard. The machine, in turn, gives you a printed reply. But the science has gone much further. It will soon be entirely possible to hold conversations with the computer on any of a variety of subjects. (Really, just like in the movie "2001.") [1]

So—build a large statue, put a talking computer inside it and—Lo! You've got a talking statue. No problem at all. Indeed, I wonder if this statue will be programmed to speak in many different tongues, also, thus imitating the events of Pentecost when all who listened to the Apostles understood although people speaking many different languages were present. Of course, all of this will have to happen in the near future if people are going to be amazed and deceived by a talking statue!

The following point is conjectural—but: given the fact that Anti-Christ is at his capital—Rome and—given the fact that Anti-Christ and Anti-Pope are working hand in glove to foster and promote the worship of Satan (for that is what is involved here)—it is quite possible this image of Anti-Christ will be manufactured in Rome and, indeed, the Vatican. Perhaps the first home of this idol will be St. Peter's itself. It is, I think, an interesting possibility.

In any case, the false worship of the beast, Anti-Christ, is forced upon the people he has under his control. The Anti-Pope has those who refuse to worship the idol killed. Timewise, in our discussion, we are now at a point just about three and a half years prior to Armageddon and the Second Coming.

It is at about this time that Anti-Christ sets out to attack Egypt yet a second time. We do not know the reasons, but we do know that Egypt is attacked a second time (Dan. 11:29). Anti-Christ, once again, attacks Egypt (Dan. 11:21–31) with all the implements of modern warfare, the massing of his men along his southern border, bringing up the tanks, the armament, the attacks by air and sea. We are all quite familiar with warfare and need no lessons as to the

---

[1] Another possibility, the hologram; the art and science of holography is making rapid progress.

mounting of a war. So, then, Anti-Christ attacks. This second time around, however, things do not turn out so well. This time the ships of Kittim will come against Anti-Christ. He will be afraid to continue his drive against Egypt and he will turn, in a fury I'll wager, against Israel. I note, in passing, that the forces of Kittim must represent some formidable western naval power. Just what nation or military power is being referred to by the word "Kittim"? It is not possible to say; many scholars feel that the name refers to Cyprus, which is an interesting possibility since England, apparently, still maintains naval bases in that island. The event is clear, however. Anti-Christ invades Israel with his military might. Even as Russia occupied Hungary back in the fifties, by way of example. Thus it is that Anti-Christ will violate his treaty with Israel.

But Anti-Christ does quite a bit more than violate a treaty. At this point he will decide to set up his image in the temple in Jerusalem, thus doing away with sacrifice and oblation to the One True God. To this end Anti-Christ enters Jerusalem and sets up his headquarters there and establishes his control of and authority over the city. (In much the same manner as any conqueror. For example, the Germans in Paris, Napoleon in Rome, or the British, Americans, and Russians in Berlin. Visualize the scene thusly.) Anti-Christ desires to crush the captive people (the Jews) of Jerusalem completely under his heel. To do this he hits upon a familiar idea. He will place his image, the now famous speaking replica, in the Holy of Holies, in the Temple which once housed the Ark of the Covenant. He has Anti-Pope arrange the triumphal entry of his image into the Holy City. As David once brought the Ark of the Covenant to Jerusalem in procession, with music and great fanfare, so now, I should think, it will be with great fanfare and acclaim, with all the citizens of the city gathered along the processional route, that the image of Anti-Christ will be brought to the Temple to be placed with great solemnity and public adoration in the Holy Place.

The Abomination of Desolation!

Now is the time when the temple shall be trodden under foot by the gentiles for forty-two months. Now is the time of Jacob's Troubles. Know, now, that the end is near.

Part II

The Time of Jacob's Troubles

So far as can be reasonably determined, the Anti-Christ will have military headquarters set up in Jerusalem. Surely Anti-Pope will be in Jerusalem not only guiding and controlling civic and money matters, apparently, but also very definitely controlling matters pertaining to religion. The populace, by and large, will be induced to offer worship before the image of the Anti-Christ. However, as it is recounted in Daniel, in these final three and a half years of Anti-Christ's empire, some among the people—i.e., the Israelites—will stand firm and refuse to offer idolatrous worship to the speaking idol standing in the holy place. Thus we are told, in Daniel, "that some of the Jewish people will die by the sword or by fire. Some will be taken captive and sold into slavery" (Dan. 11:33). The Israelites, it would seem, will receive some sort of limited help from others, i.e., militant groups I would think. However, these, too, will suffer the same fate. (If you will consult the following Scripture texts you'll understand why I refer so directly and without hesitation to slavery: Joel 4:1–8; Rev. 6:15; 13:10; 13:16; 18:13; 19:18; Luke 21:24; Zech. 14:3. By the way, the numbering of chapters and verses can vary from Bible to Bible.)

During these days Anti-Christ will do whatever he wants, exalting and magnifying himself, making himself out to be God, uttering the most hideous blasphemies against the true God. It would seem that, for a time, he actually prospers. He is seemingly successful in all his endeavors. However, as Daniel points out (Dan. 11:36–39) all this is according to the Divine Providence of God, for all of Anti-Christ's blasphemies, for all his exaltation of himself and of other false deities, too, apparently. St. John tells us that mankind will be worshipping demons, and idols in these final years of this present age (Rev. 9:20). Anti-Christ will simply be acting within the Providence of God. The Holy Land will be divided up and aliens—Anti-Christ's people—will be given charge of the land, for a price, so it seems. That phrase "for a price" intrigues me. Would that be the polite Biblical expression for "political kickback"? I wonder? In any event it is clear that gentiles will be ruling over the Holy Land and the Israelites will be killed or sold into slavery. A great number of Jews will be slaves in Greece, as well as in other countries and great numbers of Jews will be either slaves or in great desert concentration camps in Egypt (Deut. 28:68; Jer. 16:15), unless, of course, they choose to collaborate with the forces of Anti-Christ.

The great prophet Jeremiah speaks of these times in the thirtieth chapter of his book. Speaking of *that day* (i.e., the end-times) Jeremiah says that he has been commanded by the Lord to say that the fortunes of God's people, Judah and Israel, shall be restored. They will be brought back to the land and shall have possession of it. Yet though the land will be in Judah's and Israel's possession Jeremiah notes that Israel will suffer as she has never before suffered. There will be cries of panic, of terror. "Alas," he says, "that day is so great there is none like it; it is a time of *distress for Jacob.*" (Thus the phrase, the time of Jacob's troubles.) However, God will, in turn, break the yoke from their necks, burst their bonds, and strangers will no longer make servants of them. Beyond this, God will save Israel from afar, bring Israel and her offspring from the lands of their captivity, Jacob shall return and know quiet and ease. Furthermore, the Lord says that He will make a full end of all the nations among whom he scattered the Israelites.

Jeremiah ends that chapter with these words: In the *latter days* you will understand this.

I feel that little paragraph is self-explanatory. In any case, the same sort of statement was made in Daniel and that statement we have already discussed in some detail.

We have already seen the gospel narratives of these latter days. Given the complex picture we have to study and understand, it will not hurt to go over the Scripture texts again. I hope you've been following this commentary by reading the actual Bible texts. Thus, when I mention the fact that now I have to talk about St. Matthew's gospel, the twenty-fourth chapter, I certainly hope you will turn to that sacred text and read it, hopefully re-read it.

Our Lord tells us that when we see the disastrous abomination (i.e., the abomination of desolation) standing in the Holy Place (the Temple in Jerusalem), then:

(1) Those who are in Judea had best flee to the mountains.

(2) Anyone in his housetop should flee immediately and not even go into his house to take anything with him.

(3) Anyone working in the fields should not even stop to take his mantle.

(4) Pregnant women or women who are still nursing children (and therefore cannot flee) will suffer terribly. Again, this is a theme all of us are very familiar with. Women and children suffer horrible atrocities at the hands of an invading army.

(5) Men are to pray, moreover, that they will not have to flee during the winter or on a Sabbath. The reference is to the Jewish law which forbids extended travel on the Sabbath.

(6) However, at this time all mankind will suffer, not just the Jews.

Our Lord goes on to say that there will be great tribulation throughout the world during these final three and a half years prior to His Second Coming. These tribulations include the three and a half year war of the sixth trumpet/bowl, the results of Enoch and Elijah's activities, and possibly other calamities. Drought, of a very severe nature, will definitely be widespread throughout the Mid-East, at least (Is. 19:5). This worldwide tribulation will be so great that nothing like it has yet been seen and once this has occurred nothing like it will be seen again.

Our Lord does add this note of hope. He tells us that for the sake of the elect—those who have persevered in serving the one True God, in being faithful to Him—these final days of tribulation will be shortened. Otherwise no one would survive or be saved. Our Lord, then, will come again *about* three and a half years after the abomination of desolation is set up on the Temple. He will come just a bit before that precise time. Thus, His Second Coming will be as a startling surprise since He has not chosen to tell us the precise day or hour. That Second Coming will be as the lightning which comes from the east and flashes across the sky to the west. The suddenness, the unpredictability, as well as the wide visibility are referred to. That is an easy simile to understand. If we are watching a thunderstorm we know that we will, in all likelihood, see lightning. But we do not know when the lightning will occur or where it will strike. But, as we know, when it does occur it can light up the whole sky in a blazing flash. Then we will experience the oft deafening, frightening claps of thunder.

So, the coming of Our Lord.

One final note. Our Lord also warns us that many false Christs and false prophets will arise during these final three and a half years. These men and women will be able to perform great signs and wonders. They will try to lead astray even the elect. They will say that Christ is here or there, in the wilderness, in the desert. Some may say that He has come and gone, now it's too late; the only thing to do is to follow Anti-Christ. We must not be led astray; we must not believe these agents of the Devil. We must bear with all these tribulations in patient suffering. When Our Lord does come you may be sure, as He Himself says, we will know it.

St. Luke's account of these final days is much the same as St. Matthew's. St. Mark's account is also quite similar. No other details are included in either of these.

We must make note, too, of the role angels are to play, not only in the final three and a half year period which we are now discussing, but throughout the entire ten and a half year period between the Rapture and the Second Coming. St. John gives us some of these facts in the fourteenth chapter of his Revelation. He tells us that, somehow, an angel (or angels) will proclaim the gospel to all the world. Another angel (or other angels) will tell us of the impending Second Coming and also warn us of the destruction of "Babylon," i.e., Rome. Thirdly, angels will warn against receiving the mark of the beast. This will be a *real* mark of some sort, possibly an invisible mark produced by a laser beam. Instead of carrying credit cards people, quite possibly, will themselves be human credit cards, as it were. Impossible, you say! Yet just such a system is being worked on and perfected right now.

Let us turn, next, to the eleventh chapter of Revelation. At the very beginning of this chapter we learn that the nations (i.e., the gentiles) will trample the Holy City underfoot for forty-two months (i.e., for three and a half years). During this time Our Lord's two witnesses will prophesy for a period of one thousand, two hundred and sixty days (namely, not quite three and a half years). Roughly this is three years, five months, and about ten days, using a Biblical Old Testament year of 360 days. Now, before we turn to a consideration of their apostolate, it is only natural to ask: who are these two witnesses? They are Enoch and Elijah.

As recorded in Mark 9:9–13, the three apostles, Peter, James and John, were thinking over the events of the Transfiguration where Our Lord had appeared to them in glory. Also, Elijah and Moses had appeared to them. When that prefiguring event of future glory had ended, they asked Our Lord: "Why do the scribes claim that Elijah must come first?" He told them: "Elijah will indeed come first and restore everything."

In Matthew 17:10–13, Our Lord says: "Elijah is indeed coming, and he will restore everything." Then Our Lord says: "I assure you, though, that Elijah has already come, but they did not recognize him and they did as they pleased with him. The Son of Man will suffer at their hands in the same way."

A little sorting out is called for. Our Lord is making reference to

two events. One event cannot be future and past at one and the
same time. Therefore we are dealing with two events. Elijah will
come to restore all things prior to the time when Our Lord comes in
glory (i.e., His Second Coming). St. John the Baptist has come, in
the spirit of Elijah, to proclaim the first coming of Our Lord and
even as John the Baptist suffered and died so, too, will Our Lord.
Thus Our Lord's reply makes very good sense when seen in light of
the link, the relationship, the continuation, which exists between
our redemption and our resurrection.

In Malachi, Chapter 3, Verses 23–24, we read: "Lo, I will send
you Elijah, the prophet, before the day of the Lord comes, the great
and terrible day, to turn the hearts of the fathers to their children,
and the hearts of the children to their fathers, lest I come and strike
the land with doom."

The prophet Malachi, then, tells us that Elijah is to come just
prior to the Second Coming to strive to bring the Jews back to God.
This has not yet happened. It is still future. I find it extremely
fascinating to be able to tell you that the liturgy of the Mass for the
Thursday of the eleventh week in ordinary time (Reading I, year II)
uses Sirach, Chapter 48, Verses 1–14. Why do I find this fascinating? Because, as indicated earlier in this book, the liturgy, among
other things, teaches. It is used by the true Church to instruct us in
the ways of God; it is used by the Holy Spirit to guide us on our way
to salvation. And what is the true Church now teaching; what is the
Holy Spirit telling us? That Elijah will come again!

Listen to the words: "You are destined, it is written, in time to
come to put an end to wrath *before the day of the Lord*, to turn back
the hearts of fathers toward their sons, and to reestablish the tribes
of Jacob."

Apparently Elijah's return remains a part of the Jewish religious
tradition. I have just read recently something I had not previously
known. The traditional passover meal (or Seder) includes a cup
from which no one will drink. It is known as Elijah's cup. The
reference is clear. Elijah will one day return to drink from that cup.

Enoch, as was Elijah, was taken up by God, as it says in Genesis:
"Then Enoch walked with God, and he was no longer here for God
took him" (Gen. 5:21–24). Then in Sirach, Chapter 44, Verse 16, we
have the phrase: "Enoch walked with the LORD and was taken up,
to bring conversion to the nations." This is the translation from the
Latin Vulgate. The Latin is more strongly suggestive of Enoch's
future role than various current English translations. "Enoch
placuit Deo, et translatus est in paradisum, ut det gentibus
poenitentiam." The grammatical construction is that of incomplete

action and therefore looks to a future fulfillment. By way of an aside, should you read other authors on this subject you will find many of them opt for different men. The *Scriptural* evidence, however, points to Enoch and Elijah. St. Jerome's reading of this text was the Church's official version for a millennium, I might point out. Also in his translation of the Bible, Ronald Knox gives this footnote to Sirach 44:16 about Enoch: "This is commonly interpreted by the Fathers in connection with Rev. 11:3 to the 2 olive trees, i.e., Enoch and Elijah," a witness, therefore, to the early belief of the Church.

Elijah, then, will be sent to bring conversion to the Jews and also—how he will do this, I don't know—re-establish the twelve tribes, as separate entities again, apparently.

Enoch will be sent to bring conversion to the nations, that is, the gentiles, so that all peoples of the world will, somehow, have still another chance to save their souls.

Enoch and Elijah will be granted miraculous powers. Hopefully, by their preaching, their example, their highly visible power, they will bring many people back to God and, also, prepare the Jewish people to accept Our Lord at the moment of His Second Coming. They will manage to gather a strong following. They will possess these powers: anyone who attempts to harm them will be killed by fire; they will be able to prevent any rainfall during the time they are preaching, that is, for about three and a half years; they will be able to cause plagues to come upon the earth as often as they desire; and they will be able to turn water into blood (Rev. 11:4–6).

Just consider the scene: the occupation forces; Enoch and Elijah moving through the back streets and alleys of Jerusalem gathering together insurrectionists, an underground to oppose Anti-Christ. If Anti-Christ can invoke the power of Satan who dwells in him, it seems only fitting that Enoch and Elijah should be able to call upon God to aid them in a miraculous manner according to their needs. By their preaching which, I assume, will grow in intensity and vehemence, they will reach and affect many people, including many of the Jews, and draw them to the True God. This will infuriate the leaders in Anti-Christ's empire and also those who have opted for Anti-Christ. Of course, the fact that they will be the cause of widespread drought will make them less than popular with the political and military leaders of Anti-Christ's empire.

The events of these final years now crowd in upon one another with increasing rapidity. This period during which Enoch and Elijah are preaching and striving to win converts to God is the period of the second woe. It is also the time of the sixth trumpet and bowl. During this time, as St. John tells us, the great river Euphrates dries up (as well as its tributaries, it seems). Continuing drought and plague scourge mankind. All this, it seems reasonable to assume, will be the result of the miraculous powers granted to Enoch and Elijah to cause drought and plague.

Seeing the physical tribulation afflicting and disrupting Anti-Christ's empire, seeing the growing unrest, the acts of insurrection in Israel (and perhaps elsewhere) against Anti-Christ and Anti-Pope, Egypt decides to mount a war against Anti-Christ (Dan. 11:40–43).

Now Jeremiah, in his oracles against the nations, Chapter 46, speaks of Egypt at the time of the day of the Lord. As is true of so much prophetic material, the time element is a mixed one. With clear reference to the end-times (The Day of the Lord) however, Jeremiah prophesies that Egypt shall rise up like the Nile surging forward at flood tide. At the time, Egypt and her allies—a confederation, apparently, stretching from Ethiopia to Algeria—will consider themselves strong enough, not only to attack Anti-Christ, but to achieve world conquest or dominance, at least. Egypt, in prophecy, threatens to cover the earth and to destroy the city, Jerusalem, and its people.

This *will happen* at the time appointed, you may be sure. However, as Jeremiah foretells, Egypt will be defeated. Also, as Daniel points out (Dan. 11:40), Anti-Christ retaliates with a massive war effort and drives the Egyption forces back. He enters and subdues Egypt, becoming ruler there of all her vast wealth. This entire section of North Africa will be subject to Anti-Christ. However, Egypt will be in dire straits for another reason. The drought which will dry up the river Euphrates, will dry up the Nile. Thus in Isaiah, Chapter 19, Verses 5 and 6, we are told that the waters of the Nile will be dried up, the river will be parched and dry, its canals will become foul, and the branches of the Nile will diminish and dry up. This prophecy (the Nile drying up) has not yet been fulfilled. It has never dried up during the period of human history. The time for this prophecy to be fulfilled is getting shorter. These things will come to pass. They have never yet occurred, therefore they are still future. Isaiah gave us many prophecies. Many have been fulfilled; some remain to be fulfilled. Isaiah has one little prophecy about Babylon for example which is of interest because he prophesies that "Babylon shall be overthrown by God. She shall never be inhabited, nor dwelt in from age to age" (Is. 13:19–20). A number of authors, not realizing that St. John's "Babylon" is really Rome, call for a rebuilding of Babylon. These authors have overlooked this quote, this prophecy which foretells very clearly that Babylon *will not* be rebuilt.[1]

In any event, the forces of Anti-Christ are now occupied with a crumbling regime within, insurrection in the provinces, great physical disasters, and the Egyptian war. The kings of the East decide that this is an opportune time to launch an offensive against Anti-Christ. Thus, Anti-Christ receives tidings of a threatening nature from the east and the north. These communiqués alarm him and he turns from his Egyptian campaign to meet still another threat to his empire.

These kings of the east—possibly from China and other Asian countries, possibly, also, India—lead a vast horde, two hundred million troops, equipped with all the armament of modern warfare, toward the Holy Land. The Euphrates River is, by now, nothing but a dry riverbed and presents no obstacle to the advancing armies. If you find this difficult to imagine, just consider Attila the Hun, the Scourge of God, who swept across Europe in the 5th century A.D. If Attila could achieve what he did by means of his war machine, the horse, think what these kings of the east will be able to achieve with all the wondrous war machines available today. It boggles the mind!

A reprise is in order:

(1) Three and a half years yet remain until Armageddon and the Second Coming.

(2) These three and a half years correspond to the time of the sixth trumpet/bowl, the third woe in Revelation, the last half of Daniel's seventieth week.

(3) Anti-Christ's empire, beset by the physical tribulations which are manifestations of God's holy wrath, is in serious disarray and starting to crumble.

(4) Anti-Christ very probably is having trouble with many of his subject people; as is usually the case in nations occupied by foreign forces, many—perhaps most—of the people collaborate with Anti-Christ; others, small groups of people, rebel, offer resistance of one sort or another.

(5) Certainly insurgents are the cause of serious difficulties for Anti-Christ and/or his forces in Jerusalem.

(6) Anti-Christ's image is now being worshipped in the Temple. Anti-Christ wishes to be a god, he wishes to be *the* true God. Also, I suspect, on a natural level Anti-Christ has serious need of deeply devoted and faithful followers. As with the Roman emperors of old,

---

[1] See also Jeremiah 50:39–40; 51:64.

loyalty to the state will be obtained and sustained by having his subjects offer suitable worship before his statue. Also, does this point to a felt inadequacy, an inferiority complex for which he is overcompensating?

(7) Having abolished sacrifice and oblation in the Temple of Jerusalem, having established his own cult in that same temple, Anti-Christ (and perhaps, Anti-Pope) returns to Rome.

(8) Enoch and Elijah appear in Jerusalem. They go about the city preaching of the one True God and performing certain miracles as testimony to what they are saying.

(9) Egypt attacks Anti-Christ.

(10) Egypt is defeated and brought under Anti-Christ's yoke.

(11) Anti-Christ hears of armies approaching his empire from the east and the north.

(12) He hastens toward the Holy Land and sets up military headquarters near Jerusalem.

(13) Because of the drought caused by Enoch and Elijah the Euphrates is nothing but a dry riverbed, as is the Nile. The approaching horde will cross this barrier with no difficulty.

(14) The huge armies (200,000,000) will devastate the countryside. One-third of all mankind will be killed. I hardly need mention what will happen to women and girls who happen to be in the path of these relentlessly advancing armies of the east. Women and young girls will be mercilessly raped, ravished. That these invading troops might even vent their lusts upon boys and men would not surprise me in the least.

(15) It is possible that a revived Russia will be the military force attacking Anti-Christ from the north; it is also possible that the kings of the east first attack a still devastated desolate Russia and attack Anti-Christ from the north, i.e., by way of Russia.

(16) Time-wise, we are now considering the very last events which will be occurring during that final year prior to Armageddon. Keep it clearly in mind that all the events—the wars, the famine, the disease, the armies attacking and counterattacking, the eerie darkness covering the earth—all these things lead up to and are a part of that great final battle. They take place over the last three and a half years of Anti-Christ's reign, three and a half years of warfare which ends, finally, at Armageddon.

In St. John's Revelation, Chapter 16, Verses 13–14, we are told that three demons (foul spirits, like frogs) go forth from Satan, from Anti-Christ, from Anti-Pope to assemble ALL the kings of the earth for the final battle which will destroy all mankind, for that now is Satan's purpose. If Satan can destroy all mankind, and most especially the Jews and the nation Israel, the meaning of, the substance of Our Lord's Second Coming will be totally vitiated. Rev. 11:18: "It is time to destroy those who are destroying the earth." In the Greek the phrase "destroying the earth" could just as well be "destroying the land"—Israel. Satan may not be able to wipe out all mankind (e.g., some troglodytes in New Guinea might escape) but he may attempt to wipe out all Jews. Shades of Herod! Now with an increasing frenzy surely verging on insanity, Anti-Christ vents his rage upon the remaining Jews, scattering them throughout his empire, sending them into captivity, possibly into concentration camps in Egypt and elsewhere, selling them as slaves to be used in his army, or in ordinary domestic duties, selling the younger and more attractive women to be used either in houses of prostitution or for private sexual usage, selling boys and young men as male prostitutes, again, for use either in houses of male prostitution or to men and/or women on a private individual basis for sexual use and/or abuse. (Not a figment of my imagination, by the way. See Joel 4:3.) Anti-Christ will use the Jewish people for any and every infamous desire he can devise. The infamies of Nazi Germany will be as nothing compared to the fury Anti-Christ will unleash against the Jews.

At this point I do not know how to convey to you the convulsive frenzy of the time, the earth convulsed in paroxysms of hatred; the actual moment of Armageddon is at hand. Jerusalem has, by now, become an armed camp. Insurgents, led by Enoch and Elijah, attack military posts manned by the forces of Anti-Christ. They must be enjoying some success for, as St. John tells us (Rev. 11:7), Anti-Christ and his forces counterattack. Enoch and Elijah are killed. Their bodies will lie in the streets of Jerusalem for three and a half days. Men of all the peoples, tribes, tongues and nations will look at the dead bodies and refuse to let them be placed in a tomb. All those who dwell on the earth will make merry, exchange gifts. They are delighted and they exult. Why? These two men were a torment to them.

I would note—once again, I believe—that all St. John speaks of—huge armies, descriptions which bring to mind the weapons and the armament of modern warfare, worldwide participation in the events of a given area made possible by present-day sophisticated communications systems, our highly efficient spy-planes—all these things—thought to be impossible just fifty years ago—are today not only possible but already in use and accepted as common, quite ordinary everyday occurrences.

But to continue with the order of events. Enoch and Elijah will be brought back to life. The breath of life enters them and they stand upon their feet. Those who see this will experience a terrible dread and fear. Enoch and Elijah then hear a loud voice which says: "Come up here" (Rev. 11:12). Thereupon, they go up to heaven in a cloud. At precisely that moment there is an earthquake. One-tenth of the city is destroyed, seven thousand people are killed, the rest of the populace of the city is terrified and promptly give glory to the God of heaven.

The scene is easy to imagine. Probably most of you have either seen or heard about two fairly recent movies which deal in a most graphic manner with an earthquake and a skyscraper fire. ("Earthquake" and "The Towering Inferno" were the titles, I think.) Anyway, put those two pictures together and you have the picture of what it will be like in Jerusalem at this time.

Now the third woe begins, the time of the seventh trumpet/bowl. So many texts of the prophetic Scriptures deal with this climactic event that it is difficult to know where to start. I suppose the best place, after all, is the Book of Revelation. In Revelation, Chapter eleven, when that seventh trumpet sounds, voices are heard in heaven: "The kingdom of the world has become the Kingdom of Our Lord and of his Christ, and he shall reign for ever and ever." The twenty-four elders fall upon their faces and worship God, and they say:

> "We praise you, the Lord God Almighty
> Who is and who was.
> You have begun your reign.
> The nations have raged in anger,
> but then came your day of wrath
> and the moment to judge the dead:
> The time to reward your servants the prophets.
> And the holy ones who revere you,
> the great and the small alike;
> The time to destroy those who lay the earth waste."
>   (Rev. 11:16–18)

Accompanying these demonstrations in heaven are flashes of lightning, voices, peals of thunder, an earthquake and heavy hail.

Revelation, Chapter sixteen, adds just a few fascinating details to that brief listing of events which occur upon earth at the moment of the sounding of the seventh trumpet. Lightning, thunder, voices, yes. But also an earthquake to end all earthquakes. Jerusalem is split into three parts. *All* the cities of the nations fall. Islands disappear beneath the seas; mountains are flattened. Great hailstones will fall upon men and men will curse God because of this fearful plague.

In Isaiah, Chapter 24, this event is described thusly:

> "For the windows on high will be opened
> and the foundations of the earth will shake.
> The earth will burst asunder,
>   the earth will be shaken apart,
>   the earth will be convulsed.
> The earth will reel like a drunkard,
>   and it will sway like a hut;
>   Its rebellion will weigh it down,
> until it falls, never to rise again."
>
> (Is. 24:18–20)

Please note most carefully now, Joel, Chapter four:

> "For near is the day of the LORD
> in the valley of decision.
> Sun and moon are darkened,
> and the stars withhold their brightness.
>   The Lord roars from Zion,
> and from Jerusalem raises his voice;
> The heavens and the earth quake,
> but the LORD is a refuge to his people,
> a stronghold to the men of Israel."
>
> (Joel 4:14–16)

The very foundations of the world are shaken, earthquake upon earthquake beyond belief. The collapse of the cities—New York, Chicago, San Francisco, Los Angeles, Boston, New Orleans, Dallas, Seattle, Washington, Atlanta—all, all the cities will crumble, collapse. Explosion, fire, fear, panic; people trapped, killed, crushed. And not just here in the United States. The United States is, in the main, on the sidelines. We are merely onlookers. The main action is in Europe and the Near East. Madrid, Bonn, Berlin, Paris, London, The Hague, Brussels, Bern, Vienna, Venice, Naples, Athens—all will be brought to ruin. Buildings aflame, people running, trying to escape, screaming. Tokyo, Bombay.

This *will* happen and during this period of time. The clashing armies, the volcanic ash, the polluted dust and debris of the cities, the darkening of sun and moon—all in dreadful eerie darkness, all gradually building to the fateful day and the last great conflict. It takes three and a half years, but bit by bit the world will be engulfed, as if by monstrous evil forces that would destroy it utterly.

You note—I omitted Rome. The destruction of Rome is graphically described by St. John. In the eighteenth chapter of his Revelation we can see Rome destroyed. Rome has, by now, become the haunt of every foul and evil spirit, of every type of foul and hateful bird. All the nations have drunk of the wine of her impure passion and the kings of the earth have committed fornication with her. The merchants of the earth have grown rich with the wealth of her wantonness. To grasp the essence of these frightening details, imagine all the perversity, the sin, the filth, the grime pervading the entire fabric of all of our cities, put them all together—ALL the crimes, sins, evil which violate ALL ten of God's commandments and you've got the picture of Rome as it will be at the end-times.

Those who are God's people and who will have been living within the confines of the city are warned—by an angel, it seems—to come out of the city lest they perish when she does. In a single day she will be destroyed by fire. The plagues of death and mourning and famine will come upon her all at once.

The kings of the earth will stand far off, afraid of her torment, watching her destruction and will cry out:

> "Alas, alas, great city that you are,
> Babylon the mighty!
> In a single hour your doom has come!"
> (Rev. 18:10)

Please keep in mind the reference we made to Jeremiah 50:39-40; 51:64, where Jeremiah prophesies that Babylon, an ancient city now in ruins, will never be rebuilt. The reference in St. John is, of course, to Rome.

Not only do the kings of the earth mourn. So, too, do the merchants. There will be no one left to buy gold, silver, precious stones, pearls, fine linen and purple garments, silk and scarlet cloth, fragrant wood of every kind, all sorts of ivory pieces and expensive wooden furniture, bronze, iron, marble, cinnamon and balm, perfume, myrrh and frankincense, wine and olive oil, fine flour and grain, cattle and sheep, horses and carriages, slaves and human lives.

We have seen this impressive list of wealth and culture and sophistication—and decay and decadence before. Now we see it crumble and vanish before our very eyes, destroyed by fire in a single hour. Small wonder that the kings and merchants of the world mourn.

Having thus graphically described for us Rome's fall, St. John then describes the scene in heaven as Our Lord now momentarily will return to this earth. The excitement St. John feels is clear and contagious.

"Then I heard what sounded like the shouts of a great crowd, or the roaring of the deep, or mighty peals of thunder, as they cried:

'Alleluia! The Lord is king, Our God, the almighty! Let us rejoice and be glad, and give him glory! For this is the wedding day of the Lamb; his bride has prepared herself for the wedding. She has been given a dress to wear made of finest linen, brilliant white.' [The linen dress is the virtuous deeds of God's saints.] The angel then said to me: 'Write this down: Happy are they who have been invited to the wedding feast of the Lamb' " (Rev. 19:1–9).

Words fail. The mind turns to music to try to convey the intensity of the moment, the emotion of it. Handel's Hallelujah chorus sung by millions of voices, Beethoven's Ninth Symphony, Tchaikovsky's 1812 Overture with an orchestra of hundreds of thousands, with all the cannons contained under the heavens to sound out upon the earth.

And the heavens open. And behold! A white horse and He Who sits upon it is called Faithful and True and in righteousness He judges and makes war.

The Lord has returned!

Armageddon!

Our Lord sets foot upon Mount Olivet, accompanied by the Saints and the one hundred and forty-four thousand who remained undefiled and chaste who had been redeemed from the earth are with him. He will then smite the nations and rule them with a rod of iron, He will tread the wine press of the fury of the wrath of God the Almighty (Rev. 19:11–21).

Anti-Christ and his armies dare to march against the King of Kings and Lord of Lords. For all the armies of the world, having engaged in minor and major battles at varied places all around the world for the past three and a half years, have gathered now at this place, Armageddon, to wage the last great fearful battle of this present age and now they are moving against Jerusalem. The entire area is one vast battlefield.

Some details, as listed in Zechariah, Chapters 13 and 14:

(1) Two-thirds of the Jewish people will perish; one-third shall be saved.

(2) All nations gathered against Jerusalem for battle (thus accomplishing the Lord's will) will have taken the city; houses will

have been plundered; women will have been ravished; half the city will have been exiled, but the rest shall not be removed from the city.

(3) These things having happened; Our Lord returns; his feet shall rest upon the Mount of Olives. This prophecy, in Zechariah 14:4, is also to be found in Acts 1:11 which states that Our Lord will return to this earth in the same manner that He left it.

(4) The Mount of Olives shall be cleft in two from east to west by a deep valley (Zech. 14:4–5).

(5) The Lord shall strike all nations that have fought against Jerusalem: their flesh shall rot while they stand upon their feet, and their eyes shall rot in their sockets and their tongues shall rot in their mouths.

(6) But also the Jews will finally know a conversion for "On that day . . . [God] will pour out on the house of David and on the inhabitants of Jerusalem a spirit of grace and petition; and they shall look on him whom they have thrust through, and they shall mourn for him as one mourns for an only son, and they shall grieve over him as one grieves over a first-born" (Zech. 12:10).

St. John gives us the outcome of that great battle:

"Next I saw an angel standing on the sun. He cried out in a loud voice to all the birds flying in mid-heaven: 'Come! Gather together for the great feast God has prepared for you! You are to eat the flesh of kings, of commanders and warriors, of horses and their riders; the flesh of all men, the free and the slave, the small and the great!' Then I saw the beast and the kings of the earth, and the armies they had mustered to do battle with the One riding the horse, and with his army. The beast (Anti-Christ) was captured along with the false prophet (Anti-Pope) who performed in its presence the prodigies that led men astray, making them accept the mark of the beast and worship its image. Both were hurled down alive into the fiery pool of burning sulphur. The rest were slain by the sword which came out of the mouth of the One who rode the horse, and all the birds gorged themselves on the flesh of the slain" (Rev. 19:17–21).

An angel comes from heaven and holds in his hand a key to the bottomless pit and a great chain. The angel seizes the devil, Satan, binds him and throws him into the pit that he can deceive the nations no longer. And Satan shall be bound in the bottomless pit for a thousand years.

Turning for a moment to Daniel 12, we are told that the angel Michael, the great prince, comes at this moment to deliver the (Jewish) people, whose names are written in the book. Many of the dead shall rise—some to shame and contempt, others to everlasting life.

The angel who binds Satan (Revelation) and Michael, the great prince (Daniel), are quite apparently one and the same individual. We have here two accounts of one incident. In Daniel we find a few extra details: the words of Daniel's book are to be kept sealed until the end-times. At that time the WISE shall understand the words of Daniel's book, none of the wicked shall be able to understand what Daniel is speaking of. St. John, on the other hand, is told NOT to seal up the prophetic words of his book for the TIME IS NEAR (Rev. 22:10–15).

Meanwhile, God's design, His plan WILL be fulfilled. Let the evil keep doing evil, let the filthy keep on being filthy, let the righteous still do right, let the holy keep on being holy. Come what may, wherever a man may be, God's plan will happen, will be fulfilled.

It is the end of the age. The Gentiles no longer tread Jerusalem underfoot. It is Armageddon, the end and the beginning. It is the end of the Church age and of the time of the Gentiles and the beginning of the Millennial Kingdom.

As Isaiah, in his sixty-sixth chapter, says:

(Our Lord) "will send survivors to the nations: to Tarshish, Put and Lud, Mosoch, Tubal and Javan, to the distant coastlands that have never heard my fame or seen my glory; and they shall proclaim my glory among the nations" (Is. 66:19).

VIII

The Millennial Kingdom

Our Lord now reigns. He is, now, ruling over the earth, having conquered evil and the source of evil, the Devil. He rules with His saints. Hopefully, that means us. We are His saints. Having chosen Him, freely, He chooses us to rule with Him. Of course, I must hasten to make that statement clear. Our Lord first chooses us (Jn. 15:16). Then we, responding in full freedom, choose Him. Having accepted that call to follow Him, having opted for Christ, Our Lord then chooses us to rule with Him in His Kingdom.

St. Paul teaches us:

"When one of you has a grievance against a brother, does he dare go to law before the unrighteous instead of the saints? Do you not know that the saints will judge the world? And if the world is to be judged by you, are you incompetent to try trivial cases? Do you not know that we are to judge angels? How much more, matters pertaining to this life!" (1 Cor. 6:1–3). RSV

Does this seem strange to you? It does to me. Yet a number of Scripture texts tell us that this is the case. It may come as a shock to you, but ruling is something good. Ruling is a *service* to others, not something to be wallowed in and gloated over (Mt. 20:25–28). Our ruling classes, by their lust for power, their greed, pride and corruption have brought the whole profession of ruling into disrepute. In the Old Testament, the kings of Israel and Judah, with rare exceptions, were evil. In the Gospels we find several uses of the phrases: "tax-collectors and prostitutes," "publicans and sinners" ("public officials and criminals," that is) (Mt. 11:19 and Lk. 7:34), so the phenomenon is nothing new. Perhaps Attila, in his humility and honesty, really did sum it up when he described his job classification: "I am the scourge of God." Most leaders, however, want to be

147

considered benefactors to mankind, despite what they do. It should
not be that way, and in the Messianic kingdom it will not be that
way. The saints will judge the world. We are also to judge angels.
All this is startling, of that no question. But can one gainsay the
Scriptures? No, of course not.

This is one of the details we are given about the Millennial Kingdom. But we are not given very much information, really. To tell
the truth, at the present time not much information is needed. Our
Lord will have returned. I am sure He will lead and guide us
according to the Divine Providence for the Millennial Kingdom.

St. John (Rev. 20:1–3), for example, relates the following facts:
Satan is thrown into the pit and sealed in that pit for a thousand
years. For reasons as of now unknown, Satan will be released from
that pit for a little while at the end of the thousand years. We can
only assume that the reason Satan is allowed to attack God's holy
people at that time will be the same as the reason he is allowed to
attack God's holy people now. People composed of body and soul,
intellect and FREE WILL must make a choice for good or evil. As we
must choose God freely over all obstacles and also material benefits, so must the inhabitants of the Millennial Kingdom.

In any case, those who were beheaded for their testimony to
Jesus and for the word of God, who had not received the mark of the
beast on their foreheads or hands, come to life and reign with the
Lord for a thousand years. So the saints, those who made the Rap-
ture and those who suffered martyrdom during the persecutions of
Anti-Christ will rule with Our Lord in His Kingdom.

St. John adds the words that this is the first resurrection and
blessed and holy is he who shares in this first resurrection. If we
share in this first resurrection the second death will have no power
over us and we shall be *priests* of God and of Christ and shall reign
with Him for a thousand years.

St. John mentions this aspect of the Kingdom much earlier in his
book of Revelation. In Revelations, Chapter 2, Verses 24–28, speaking to those of the Church in Thyatira, he says:

"He who conquers and who keeps my works until the end, I will
give him power over the nations, and he shall rule them with a rod
of iron . . ." RSV

Then, again, in Chapter 5, Verses 6–10, when Our Lord takes the
sealed scroll, the saints sing:

"Worthy art thou to take the scroll and to open its seals, for thou
wast slain and by thy blood didst ransom men for God from every
tribe and tongue and people and nation, and hast made them a
kingdom and *priests* to our God, and they shall reign on earth." RSV

The twelve apostles, it seems clear, will be sitting on thrones

judging the twelve tribes of Israel. It may be that this is what all
those who continue with Our Lord in His trials will be doing. The
verse in Luke, Chapter 22, Verse 28, reads:

"You are those who have continued with me in my trials; and I
assign to you, as my Father assigned to me, a kingdom, that you may
eat and drink at my table in my kingdom, and sit on thrones judging
the twelve tribes of Israel." RSV

I am sure most of us do not consider the parable of the ten Talents
as one to be taken in its literal sense. We are accustomed to interpreting the parable in a spiritual sense. The lesson always was: do
well with the gifts, the abilities God has given you that you may
therefore make a suitable return for the gift and, of course, thereby
save your soul. This was and *is* a sound and invaluable interpretation. The possibility exists, however, that Our Lord, in the guise of
the returned master, rewards those who are able to make a return
upon what he has given them; he is actually promising not only a
spiritual recompense but authority or the sharing of authority over
some sector of the Millennial Kingdom. Our Lord does say, about
those servants who have been faithful and who can make a return
upon that which was entrusted to them:

"Well done, good and faithful servant; you have been faithful
over a little, I *will set you over* much" (Mt. 25:21). (*See also* 2 Tim.
2:12.) Lk. 19:12–26 even says: "take over ten cities; take over five
cities!"

This message is to be found in the pages of the Old Testament as
well. Thus, in Daniel, we see the following:

"And the kingdom and the dominion and the greatness of the
kingdoms under the whole heaven shall be given to the people of
the saints of the Most High; their kingdom shall be an everlasting
kingdom, and all dominions shall serve and obey them" (Dan.
7:27). RSV

According to Daniel, then, the saints (that is, the Jews) will rule
in an everlasting kingdom and all other dominions (other nations, I
assume) shall serve and obey them.

"It shall come to pass *in the latter days* that the mountain of the
house of the Lord shall be established as the highest of the mountains and shall be raised above the hills; and all nations shall flow to
it, and many peoples shall come, and say:

" 'Come, let us go up to the mountain of the Lord, to the house of
the God of Jacob; that he may teach us his ways and that we may
walk in his paths.'

"For out of Zion shall go forth the law, and the word of the LORD
from Jerusalem.

"He shall judge between the nations, and decide for many

peoples; And they shall beat their swords into plowshares, and their spears into pruning hooks; nation shall not lift up sword against nation, neither shall they learn war any more" (Is. 2:2–4). RSV

This text from the Old Testament and a number of others deal with the Millennial Kingdom. However, the texts deal primarily with Israel's role in that kingdom. The message of the prophet Ezekiel deals rather exclusively, I should say, with the Jewish nation. Thus, in Ezekiel, Chapter 36, we find that God announces His plans to return the Israelites to the land. God plans to bring them again to a true worship of Himself in spirit and truth. In our Easter Liturgy, we apply that to ourselves and our spiritual life, of course. This is to the good, but the prophecy will have a literal fulfillment as well.

In Ezekiel, Chapter 37, a startling prophecy is made. Judah and Ephraim (Israel) shall become one. The Jewish nation, once split in two, will be one. They will be one nation and will be returned to the land of Jacob. Israel and Judah shall be one kingdom (Ezek. 37:15–28). They shall offer a true and holy worship to God and God will dwell with them forever. Moreover, Ezekiel prophesies, in two places—Chapters 34 and 37—that David shall be king over Israel forever and God will set His Sanctuary in their midst. (I will make no comment upon these two texts since I suspect they deal not with the Millennial Kingdom but with Eternity—that is, God's eternal kingdom at the culmination of the thousand year reign of Our Lord.)

Since Israel is to become the seat of power in the Messianic Kingdom, with Jerusalem as the world capital, the question arises: Will all the world become a West Bank? Will everyone live in a Gaza strip? The answer is no. We must not imagine the future Israel to be modeled on the present state by that name.

Ezekiel tells us that the nation must first be gathered in unbelief. This is going on now. Later, after the Russian invasion, the Spirit of God will be poured out on all, but especially Israel, and they will be converted to God. For a short time prior to the persecution of the Jews which Anti-Christ will institute, they, or at least a significant number of them, will observe God's laws. These include the command not to "molest the foreigner in your midst, for you were once foreigners in Egypt" (Ex. 22:20); Deut. 10:19 even commands that one is to "love the stranger in your midst" and Deut. 24:14–15 orders one not to "exploit the stranger in the town." If these commands were now being carried out, life in the occupied territories would be more bearable, and perhaps there would be peace in the area now. Peace is the fruit of justice. What is going on now is causing God's name to be blasphemed among the nations, as Ezekiel would put it (Ezek. 36:22). Too, "Be sure that it is not for any goodness of yours that Yahweh gives you this rich land, for you are a headstrong people" (Deut. 9:6). No, it is being done by God in faithfulness to His promises.

But in the Millennial Kingdom, the Jews will have accepted Christ. Only one-third of the nation will have done so, but this is the fraction that survives Armageddon. Then, with Jesus the Messiah ruling, Christian principles will prevail. Unfortunately they have never yet been put into practice on an appreciable scale in any country. When they are, this world will become a paradise.

Of the Millennial Kingdom not much else can be said. That the kingdom will be established is crystal clear. That the nations will serve the Lord is, again, clear. Wars will cease, the Jews will be regathered from many nations. Too, the Jewish people will be converted to Our Lord. Thus, in Isaiah we have this fascinating prophecy:

"In that day there will be a highway from Egypt to Assyria, and the Assyrian will come into Egypt, and the Egyptian into Assyria, and the Egyptians will worship with the Assyrians.

"*In that day* Israel will be the third with Egypt and Assyria, a blessing in the midst of the earth, whom the Lord of hosts has blessed, saying, 'Blessed be Egypt my people, and Assyria the work of my hands, and Israel my heritage' " (Is. 19:23–25). RSV

After Armageddon, the first order of business will be to make the earth habitable again. Things will be a mess at the start, the place littered with corpses, debris from dwellings, landslides, mud, volcanic ash and smoldering lava. Food may be a problem for a while (except for the vultures) until things start growing again. Dan. 12:12–13 indicates this period will last 45 days.

Meanwhile survivors from Armageddon (there will be some, cf. Zech. 14:16) start the long trek home. When they find the ruins of their former homes, they tell the survivors there the news of the great battle (Is. 66:18–19). These survivors will be those believers in God who came through the great Church persecution, those who heeded the later messages of the angels (Rev. 14:9–12), and the few who were converted when they experienced the terrors of the final days. Their number is small. Figures scattered throughout the Book of Revelation indicate that *at the most* one quarter of those around after the Rapture survive to Armageddon. But others, an unspecified number, also die in plagues and judgments, where no numbers are given. Presumably, few children are born during this time.

How many finally survive depends on how many lived good moral lives during this time, or finally came to believe in God, or at least showed kindness to the persecuted Christians and Jews (Mt. 25: 31–46). We are not given any statistics on this, but the final numbers should delight and gratify the Zero Population Growth advocates.

At the Rapture, only those in sanctifying grace were taken up. (Even I am writing in the prophetic perfect now. It's still future, as of 1976!) Here, following Armageddon, to remain on earth it seems sufficient to have performed some overt act of disloyalty to Anti-Christ. We can only speculate on this. The Scriptures are not that clear about this point. Apparently many will be pleasantly surprised to find themselves spared. God's mercy doesn't fail, even at a time like this. After all (Wis. 1:13) "Death is not God's handiwork, He takes no pleasure in destroying the living."

This section of Matthew's gospel (Mt. 25:33) actually refers to the final judgment, but Armageddon is a "type" for it. There is a separation of the sheep from the goats. The sheep are obviously the flock of the Good Shepherd. The goats are the followers of Satan. Devil worship traditionally includes worshipping Satan's symbol: the goat of Baphomet. The "goats" are now disposed of (cf. also Lk. 13:27). We know Mt. 25:31 refers to the final judgment, because the evil go to Hell, the good to everlasting life. The greek word aionion can mean "for an age," and this would be appropriate for the ones who survive Armageddon. However, the New Testament uses this same word in the sense of "everlasting" in other places. Therefore the primary meaning of this judgment scene is the final (white throne) judgment; but Armageddon is a type of this, insofar as it also involves the separation of sheep and goats, the goats to hellfire, the sheep to life. All men are supposed to be "sheep," but some degenerate into "goats."

The next order of business will be the final return of the Jews to their homeland. Prophecies on this now have to be fulfilled completely. A start on this occurred after the Russian debacle, but it was interrupted, and even reversed during Anti-Christ's persecution of the Jews. Now it can be completed. Many Jews also died during the preceding years, but one-third have survived (Zech. 13:8). These now believe, not only in God, but in Jesus Christ also, making them, technically, Christians.

Tarshish has survived and has ships, for these are now used in bringing some Jews home (Is. 60:8–9). Airplanes also are apparently still around. But other modes of transportation are also used (Is. 66:20–21). Gentiles will now delight in aiding the Jews' return, and consider it an honor to help rebuild the country (Is. 60:1–22; *also* Is. 49:1–26). This return will henceforth be considered *the*

great event in Israel's history, overshadowing even the Passover
(Jer. 16:15). Israel will be prosperous, peaceful and happy at last
(Is. 60:18–22). We are told some of the details of the geography of
Israel (it will be much larger than now) and something about the
new temple and social arrangements. Architects and liturgists interested in this will find a description in Ezekiel, Chapters 40 to 48.
The geography and climate of the earth will have been considerably changed by then, mountains being leveled, the oceans having
different borders, and national boundaries having long since been
radically altered, so we had best not speculate too much about
these things here. For all mankind it will be a time of peace, prosperity and joy.

What happens to the Church (the true one), or rather its remnants
at this time? We are not told. But Jesus does tell us (Mt. 28:20):
"And know that I am with you all days; yes, to the end of the age."
Now He takes over.

The earth will be made new, a process that will take a thousand
years. Isaiah's description of this in his 65th chapter is the culmination of the thousand year reign of Our Lord when He will present
the kingdom to His Father:

"For behold, I create new heavens and a new earth; And the former
things shall not be remembered or come into mind. But be glad and rejoice
forever in that which I create; for behold, I create Jerusalem a rejoicing,
and her people a joy. I will rejoice in Jerusalem, and be glad in my people;
no more shall be heard in it the sound of weeping and the cry of distress.

"No more shall there be in it an infant that lives but a few days, or an old
man who does not fill out his days, for the child shall die a hundred years
old, and the sinner a hundred years old shall be accursed.

"They shall build houses and inhabit them; they shall plant vineyards
and eat their fruit.

"They shall not build and another inhabit; they shall not plant and
another eat; for like the days of a tree shall the days of my people be, and
my chosen shall long enjoy the work of their hands.

"They shall not labor in vain, or bear children for calamity; for they shall
be the offspring of the blessed of the LORD, and their children with them.

"Before they call I will answer, while they are yet speaking I will hear.

"The wolf and the lamb shall feed together, the lion shall eat straw like
the ox; and dust shall be the serpent's food.

"They shall not hurt or destroy in all my holy mountain, says the LORD"
(Is. 65:17–25). RSV

Turning, again, to St. John's Revelation, Chapter 20, we find that
when the thousand year reign of Christ is ended, Satan is loosed
from his bonds for a little while. He will deceive the nations once
again, and specifically, again, for a second time, Gog and Magog. (I

think it would be unwise to speculate on just what or who is being referred to since this prophecy is very far in the future, indeed.) It is best, here, simply to say, with St. John, that the nations will, again, gather to do battle with the saints, to march against the Holy City. This time around, these armies are destroyed by fire. Satan is now thrown into the lake of fire and sulphur where Anti-Christ and Anti-Pope are. They will be tormented day and night for ever and ever.

Then comes the great white throne judgment. Then ALL the dead (those who rose earlier are not included, "the second death shall have no power over them") are brought back to life and are judged according to their deeds. Death and Hades are then thrown into the lake of fire as well as all those whose names are not found in the book of life.

Then it is that St. John sees a new heaven and a new earth. He sees a new Jerusalem coming down out of heaven from God:

"And he who sat upon the throne said, 'Behold, I make all things new.' Also he said, 'write this, for these words are trustworthy and true.' And he said to me, 'It is done! I am the Alpha and the Omega, the beginning and the end. To the thirsty I will give from the fountain of the water of life without payment. He who conquers shall have this heritage, and I will be his God and he shall be my son. But as for the cowardly, the faithless, the polluted, as for murderers, fornicators, sorcerers, idolators, and all liars, their lot shall be in the lake that burns with fire and sulphur, which is the second death'" (Rev. 21:5–8). RSV

The Heavenly Jerusalem glitters as a jewel and the glory of God is its light. In it there is no Temple for the Temple is the Lord God Almighty and the Lamb. And God will be everything to everyone.

"But Christ has in fact been raised from the dead, the first fruits of all who have fallen asleep. Death came through one man and in the same way the resurrection of the dead has come through one man. Just as all men die in Adam, so all men will be brought to life in Christ; but all of them in their proper order: Christ as the first-fruits and then, after the coming of Christ, those who belong to him. After that will come the end, when he hands over the kingdom to God the Father, having done away with sovereignty, authority and power. For he must be king until he has put all his enemies under his feet and the last of the enemies to be destroyed is death, for everything is to be put under his feet. Though when it is said that everything is subjected, this clearly cannot include the One who subjected everything to him. And when everything is subjected to him, then the Son himself will be subject in his turn to the One who subjected all things to him, so that God may be all in all" (1 Cor. 15:20–28). JB

IX

An Exhortation
"What to do"

In our study of the end-times, the latter days, we have covered a good bit of territory and a massive amount of information. Yet all the subjects, all the material, all the details can be summed up under five headings:

(1) Preliminary Signs.
(2) The Rapture, the First Great Sign.
(3) The Plagues, the Second Great Sign.
(4) Armageddon.
(5) The Second Coming.

Under preliminary signs we studied:

(1) The destruction of the Temple.
(2) The beginning of the return of the Jews to the Land.
(3) The rebuilding of the Temple.
(4) The trouble of many false messiahs.
(5) War, rumors of wars, famine.
(6) The Apostasy.
(7) Peace and security for a time.
(8) As it was in the days of Noah and Lot.
(9) The ten nation confederacy.
(10) Russia ready and willing to invade Israel.
(11) Prophecies become clear.
(12) Anti-Christ is around but is not yet recognized.

We then studied, in detail, the Rapture, the first of the great signs. Following upon our study of the Rapture, we discussed:

(1) Seal one—imperialism.
(2) Seal two—wars.
(3) Seal three—inflation, famine.

(4) Seal four—death, plagues.
(5) Seal five—the martyrs—those who die for Our Lord.
(6) The problem of Gog and Magog, the Russian invasion of Israel, seal six.
(7) Seal seven—a pause in heaven, the spiritual revival and the return of the Jews.
(8) The firm covenant.

Then we considered the second of the great signs, the plagues (the trumpets/bowls):

(1) Plagues one, two, three, four and five.
(2) The time of Jacob's troubles.
(3) Wars—up to the final great war, Armageddon, plague six.
(4) The Second Coming.

The details we have studied could also be summarized this way:
The first great sign—the Rapture, when the Good Shepherd leads his flock, those who are ready, out of harm's way.

The seals—when Christ claims the inheritance He has repurchased, while Satan instead tries to usurp the earth. During this time the strays in the flock are being gathered. This culminates in Russia trying to seize the center of what is to be Christ's headquarters and Russia is soundly defeated and repulsed.

The seven-year treaty—where Anti-Christ usurps God's place as Israel's protector. Once this occurs, God counterattacks sending seven warning plagues on the world, the second great sign that He means to be in control. The nations react by gathering at Armageddon, to destroy Israel, and if possible prevent Christ's return.

Christ returns in power and majesty as He promised, and finally sets up His Kingdom, whose capital Jerusalem becomes the world capital, and destroys those who were destroying the land.

When Christ started His public ministry He got up in the synagogue at Nazareth, His home town (Lk. 4:16), took the scroll and read the following two verses from Isaiah (61:1–2):

"The Spirit of the Lord is upon me, because He has anointed me to preach the good news to the poor. He has sent me to proclaim release to the captives and recovering of sight to the blind, to set at liberty those who are oppressed, to proclaim the acceptable year of the Lord." RSV

Then He announced that this prophecy was now fulfilled. He left out the last phrase of Verse 2: "A day of vengeance for our God." Now at Armageddon, the complete fulfillment has occurred, and

His kingdom is now literally established. This is what happens, this is what He does. What are *we* to do?

Since a number of the preliminary signs we have studied are very evident, clearly present—in our view, NOW is the time to prepare. We have seen the text a number of times, that we know not the day or the hour. Therefore in looking toward the latter days and the Second Coming a word to the wise suffices.

Keep in mind these points:

(1) All non-preliminary events begin after the Rapture, which is the first great sign. It involves the Church. "Judgment begins in the house of God" (1 Pt. 4:17).

(2) You have known about Christ's Second Coming all along. You have known about the Rapture—the rising of the just dead, and the transformation of the good to heavenly glorified bodies all along. The only surprising thing is that these two events are not separated by only a few minutes, but that according to the Scriptures, there is a period of approximately 10½ years between these two events. This is the time span I have been trying to fill out for you.

(3) The prophecies are like scattered parts of a jigsaw puzzle, spread throughout the Scriptures. When they are finally fitted together, a clear pattern finally begins to emerge.

(4) At the judgment the sheep will be separated from the goats. Sheep represent the flock of Christ. The goats are aptly followers of Satan, who have traditionally worshiped a goat, Baphomet.

(5) The end of this age means the Second Coming, not the Rapture. It ends when Jerusalem is no longer trodden underfoot by the Gentiles. This is the Coming.

(6) "The Lord does not delay in keeping his promise—though some consider it "delay." Rather, he shows you generous patience, since he wants none to perish but to come to repentance" (2 Pt. 3:9).

BE PREPARED

Be prepared, in the first place, for the Rapture.[1] The Rapture, as you now know, occurs about ten and a half years before the actual

[1] At the time of the Rapture there will be much confusion and particularly so right after. Millions of persons will be missing. Homes will be uninhabited, classrooms—particularly elementary ones—will be empty, offices and shops disrupted by absentees. There will be problems about inheritances and insurance policies. Has the testator legally died? Will unclaimed property escheat to the state,

moment of the Second Coming. No one knows the day or the hour
of the Rapture. Why? If it were possible to determine that the
Rapture would occur, for example, on Dec. 24, 1977, between 9 and
10 P.M., EST, people would then say: "Let's eat, drink and be merry
right up to Christmas Eve. Then we'll run over to the Church and
go to confession!" No wonder God does not reveal to us the exact
day or hour of the Rapture! However, all the members of Our
Lord's Mystical Body in the state of Sanctifying Grace will be
caught up to be with the Lord always. The key phrase is "in the
state of Sanctifying Grace."

I think that, as practicing Catholics, you know how to achieve
that state. You know you are supposed to obey *all* of God's commandments, first of all. If we are neglecting any, or even one, of His
commandments we cannot be in the state of Grace. So the first step
in preparing for the Rapture is to review our life and see if we are
neglecting, in one way or another, one of God's Ten Commandments. I would take this opportunity to remind you that there are
ten commandments and all must be observed.

In the second place, to prepare for the Rapture, you should strive
to lead a sacramental life. As Catholics we still have the obligation
to attend Sunday Mass. We still should receive the sacrament of
penance at reasonably frequent intervals, and as soon as possible
should we commit a mortal sin. We still have a serious obligation to
receive Holy Communion, again at reasonably frequent intervals,
but we should receive often—every week, even every day, if that
be possible.

The Church no longer has religious penitential norms. However,
we should practice something in the way of penance on our own.
We do not have to do anything extraordinary. But all can practice
fast and abstinence—and other penances—in an inconspicuous
small way. This is very pleasing to God because we are trying to do
something, very quietly and privately, to please Him and to atone
for our sins and the sins of others.

Then, thirdly, to prepare for the Rapture you really should lead a
reasonably active prayer life. We ought to say some vocal prayers
on a regular daily basis. We should spend a little time at the very
least thinking *about* God—or even better, just being *with* Him and
doing nothing else. We should really work at being with God all the

or to next of kin, or to—? If things are left to Church organizations, will they belong
to the true or to the new harlot church? Who will take care of orphaned teen-agers?
These are practical problems. Not being legal or financial counselors, only spiritual
ones, we have no answers. We only indicate some of the problems and leave solu-
tions to you.

day long so that finally we come to realize that no matter what we are doing, no matter where we are, God is with us and in us, Our Lord is with us and in us.

Prayer is essential. We are told to pray always, so that as a result we will escape the things that are to come (Lk. 21:36). But prayer and sacrifice are not just for ourselves. As members of Christ's Mystical Body, we pray for each other, and for those who are not yet members of that body. We know of the hardships and catastrophes that are to come. They cannot be averted. But their severity may be mitigated by our prayers. Souls can be saved. Martyrs need grace to become shining examples and give greater glory to God. The wicked, even the persecutors can be converted and saved. These are certainly things to be prayed for. We need not just look on passively. Jesus said of Himself (Jn. 9:4): "As long as it is day I must carry on the work of Him who sent me." And this should be a model for us. Only of two people's salvation must we despair: Anti-Christ and the Anti-Pope. We are told they go to Hell. But everyone else's salvation can still be hoped for, prayed for, and sacrificed for. (Sacrifice is after all a non-verbal form of prayer.) Here then is something for us to aim for. And by helping others, we assure our own salvation (cf. James 5:19–20).

If we will but practice all three of these suggestions on a regular basis we will always be well prepared for the Rapture.

As we have said, one of the preliminary signs of the Rapture is the Apostasy. Once this occurs the time of the Rapture will surely be close. Therefore once you realize the Apostasy has occurred be sure to adhere to all the spiritual principles we have suggested most assiduously.

Follow the true Church. You will be able to tell the true Church from the false "harlot" church. That faction which adheres to and maintains the faith of our fathers, is true to the moral and spiritual truths enunciated through the ages—this will be the true Church. That faction which deviates from the faith of our fathers, becomes more permissive, more humanistic, more rationalistic, emphasizes man at the expense of God—this will be the false "harlot" church.

Follow the true Church. Stay in the state of Grace. Try to prepare and warn others of the approaching Rapture, and the approach of the latter days and all that that entails. If you find it difficult to preach openly to others about these matters, then I would suggest giving copies of this book to others, to people liable to be around after the Rapture. (You'll be doing them a very great spiritual favor, believe me!)

Continue in your normal activities—but don't make any long

range plans. These principles are always good, but after the apostasy they become desperately urgent.

AT THE MOMENT OF THE RAPTURE, answer that call instantly and joyously, as we indicated earlier in this book.

If you are left behind AFTER THE RAPTURE (and that could be any one of us, after all), you have two choices: a firm stand for God or an accepting of the mark of the beast.

Should we take a firm uncompromising stand for God we will probably become martyrs (by being beheaded, very likely) and thereby, of course, achieving the glory of heaven. We are told that should we be imprisoned and suffer during the persecution of the true Church, we will be told what to say when we are dragged before judges or into synagogues. The Holy Spirit will supply the words, so we have no worry on that account. But be aware that we are also told that family members may turn against us in this time of persecution. Of course, whether this persecution will occur in the United States is something that is open to question. It is, at least, a possibility. Also open to question is whether or not you would have to receive the mark of the beast were you to decide for Satan and *against* God, here in the United States. It is, I suppose, a possibility. In any case, should we opt for Satan, we will live in relative safety and comfort. However, once the plagues start coming, we will be killed off and go to Hell.

So—in the long run that is what it all boils down to, Heaven or Hell and the choice is yours. Your life expectancy, now—after the Rapture—is ten and a half years, at most, before you would end up in Hell.

All I can say is that if you do give in because of human weakness, and deny God then repent *immediately*. Since the true Church will probably disappear you will not have the opportunity to receive the sacraments.

You should certainly avoid the serious sins that will be rampant at this time. For example, abortion will be a raging epidemic. But this is a serious sin, condemned by God's commandment. This is the teaching of the True Church. The very earliest documents testify to the constant teaching of the Church on this matter. Two documents, the Didache and the Letter of Barnabas, which date back to the first century of this present church age, tell us: "Do not murder a child by abortion, nor kill it at birth" and "Do not murder a child by abortion, nor, again, destroy that which is born."

I would add that these documents, reflecting the mind of the true Church of the first century, also state, clearly and succinctly: "Do not be sexually promiscuous. Do not commit adultery. Do not be sexually perverted (literally translated, this reads: do not be a corrupter of children/boys)." In his translation and comparative study of the Didache and Barnabas, Kraft notes that this phrase "do not be a corrupter of children/boys" refers specifically to that homosexual misconduct in which *young men* are adapted for the female sexual role, thereby "corrupting" their natural sexual functions, and often leading to castration or, so it was believed, to impotence. But the term also includes, in its meaning, sodomy/homosexuality *in general*.

These sins are mentioned here because they are suggested in the Book of Revelation. Idolatry, drugs and thefts are also mentioned. Murder includes euthanasia, too, and that's beginning to be popular. This may spread from the sick and elderly to the mentally defective, then to the socially undesirables, including Christians, Jews and other "traitors to mankind." The best you can do is to withdraw very quietly from society in general, stay away from other religious services offered by the harlot church and, on your own, stay close to God as best you can. Pray frequently; Grace is still available; you are not abandoned by God. Nevertheless life will now be very difficult. You have a one in four chance to survive until the Coming, but don't gamble on it. At least you know the Second Coming is not far off.

I must also warn you that during this time a number of people will be around claiming visions from God, even working miracles. Believe all these messages only if they correspond to the teachings of the True Church, because numerous *false* prophets will be around to try and mislead you.

St. Paul tells us (1 Tim. 4:1–4) that in the *last days* some will claim to have visions and teach that marriage is forbidden and also to abstain from certain foods. This is already being taught in some communes today (for reasons of their own). But then the teaching will probably be more like this: "It's too late now, let's not bring any more children into this world. Too, when Israel will be re-established, the dietary laws will bind everyone, so practice them now to obtain salvation!" This sounds like Satan's ruse: since infants are now all safe—not one of them can lose heaven or sanctifying grace, certainly not before they are 10 years old—and that's all the time that's left—make sure there are as few as possible; and as for adults—make them rely for salvation not on God, or on grace, but on some external work, preferably something like dietary laws which are useless for them. We have been warned by Paul about this some 1900 years ago already.

At the time of the SIGNING OF THE TREATY between Anti-Christ and Israel (this is something you already know about, again) the persecutions will come to an end and the time of the plagues (which we have studied, listing them under the symbols of trumpets and bowls) will start. As Christians, members of the TRUE CHURCH, we will not suffer death or serious harm. We will share in the general discomfort and material losses of the time, naturally. If we are still around we might possibly find other small groups of true believers around, here or there. If so, we would probably be wise to join them, help them, even as they probably would prove a help to us, an encouragement to us.

It may be that we will have contact with other people who, now, are finally seeking God. We would be in a position to and should offer our help, tell them they can still be saved, tell them what is going on, explain why God so punishes mankind.

Any newborn babies, or adult converts who have not previously been baptized, should be baptized. Anyone can do it, you don't even have to be baptized yourself to do it. It's easy. Pour ordinary tap water, lukewarm is more comfortable, if available, over the forehead of the one to be baptized, while saying "Jack (or Joan) (or whatever name), I baptize you in the name of the Father and of the Son and of the Holy Spirit." Nothing more. This is the simple, emergency form. Needless to say, Baptism is given only once, it is not to be repeated.

As the time of the Second Coming is quite near and the fury, the frenzy of Anti-Christ mounts in intensity, a few practical hints for day-to-day living are in order. Bear in mind that any news from official sources in Anti-Christ's kingdom will be badly slanted. It will be difficult to form a true picture of world events. For example, Anti-Christ will probably have taken credit for destroying the Russian army when it invaded Israel, taken credit for having rescued Israel from the Russian yoke. The reality, of course, is that God rescued the Jews from Russian subjugation. As you were aware of that distortion, so now, in the times after that Russian invasion, be very wary of official news bulletins. It might well be that any news about Enoch and Elijah will be censored so you may have a difficult time learning of their activities. (To tell the truth, there is nothing much new about this element of distortion of the news. Even here in the United States, our news comes to us in badly distorted fashion and, despite all protests to the contrary, is very badly slanted.)

Dodge the draft. You will not want to be part of Armageddon.

DURING THE FINAL DAYS of darkness, stay indoors, persevere in prayer. If you have any sacramentals around, use them. Don't go out searching for Our Lord. His Coming will be very evident; He will let us know, be assured.

Should we be still alive at the actual moment of the Coming, things will be rather messy for a while. But then Our Lord will reign and a glorious time will now begin. And Our Lord Himself will guide us as to what we are to do in His Millennial Kingdom.

It is natural enough to wonder at the suffering allowed by the good and gracious God. Yet the suffering to be endured in the end-times has a Divine purpose. It is a single observable phenomenon that in bad times, as wartime for example, our churches are filled. In good times, many people do not bother with church. When something goes wrong or people are in trouble, they pray. They frequently forget to pray when things are going along smoothly and they are well. The good and great God is not above allowing suffering to bring us to our knees and to seek Him above all else.

Thus, for those Christians who stay alive during these parlous times suffering will serve to purify them from attachment to things of the earth. They will then live long lives in the Kingdom.

For the Jews (and also for members of the harlot church) suffering serves as a call to conversion. Man is not in control of the earth, neither is Satan. God is. He is using the calamities, the hatred of Satan, and everything else to bring about conversions and to save souls that would otherwise have been lost. By letting Satan rampage, he is gathering a bigger flock than he could have otherwise. Satan is being used, as he was used at the Crucifixion, where he helped to bring about the Redemption.

For the wicked, suffering is the last call to repentance. They should have been sent to Hell at the Rapture. This is their last chance. They would have suffered more in Hell in the meantime, where they already deserve to be. God could have crushed them at the Rapture. After all, all of this is completely under God's control.

As for those who suffer martyrdom, bear in mind that the blood of martyrs is the seed of Christians. Also Satan now tries to crucify the Mystical Body of Christ, His human extension on earth, now that He (Christ) is in heaven. Like St. Paul, martyrs (and confessors, and the sick and the blind, etc.) fill up what is lacking in the suffering of Christ (Col. 1:24). Must not the Church also suffer and so enter into glory? Pray even for those who persecute you. As St. Paul tells us (Rom. 12:14): "Bless those who persecute you; bless them and never curse them." After all they are helping increase your glory in heaven. If you do suffer for being good, count it as a blessing (1 Pt. 3:14). Remember St. Stephen, the first martyr after Our Lord. While being stoned to death he prayed (Acts 7:60). "Lord do not hold this sin against them"—and Saul the persecutor then became the Apostle Paul. Martyrs and others who suffer for Christ are special favorites of God. Just as we venerate the marks on Jesus' hands and feet, these members of His Mystical Body who have suffered will be honored in Heaven.

I have hesitated to mention one aspect of the latter days. I have not wanted to offend my Jewish friends and/or colleagues. Then one must consider the tremendous amount of work invested in the Judeo-Christian institutes of our various universities.

However, I must, at least, mention the fact that Jews will be persecuting Catholics, and, perhaps, all Christians, during the first three and a half years following the Rapture. It would seem that Jews will join forces with Anti-Christ and all those who are persecuting the Church. Jews will be active in manhandling and persecuting us if we are caught by them. Jews will summon us to *synagogues* and prisons, bring us to trial before kings and governors—all because of Our Lord's name. St. Luke is very clear about this. See St. Luke, Chapter 21, Verses 10–19. See, in particular, Verse 12. St. Mark tells us, if we are here and alive during this three and a half year period, that should Jews get hold of us we will be beaten *in the synagogues*. This is in St. Mark, Chapter 13, Verse 9.

Of course, as you know by now, Jews will be persecuted during the time of Jacob's troubles, the final three and a half years before the Second Coming. This is, of course, a sad and terrible thing, but Jews will have been actively engaged in persecuting and killing Christians thereby setting the precedent and example for their own destruction.

Jacques Maritain points out the reason for such suffering in his *The Peasant of the Garonne.* His wife, Raissa, notes that *what is lacking in the Passion of Christ,* as St. Paul phrases it, is its development in time. Christ, now with His Father, cannot do this. *However,* this can be accomplished in His mystical body, and it is. Thus Maritain quotes Cardinal Journet as saying that the "Church of the Cross" must precede "the Church of glory."

Martyrdom, then, is the ultimate gift of man to God, and of God to men (Mt. 5:10–12). Matthew 10:17–25 lists some instructions for us, if and when we suffer persecution.

The Good Shepherd had led His flock out of danger *at the Rapture;* now the strays are being rounded up. God's providence and grace are still active, and even more so after the outpouring of the Spirit begins. All these things we have studied in some detail. You know well that, should we suffer martyrdom, the Spirit will tell us what to say, the Spirit will give us the grace of willpower and perseverance.

Throughout the history of the Church millions have already acquired the martyr's crown; now, after the Rapture, millions more will also. These are victims for Christ. We should console, help these victims, where possible, even as the early Christian martyrs helped one another. After all, Our Lord said that whatever was done to one of His least brethren was done unto Him. That is as true now as it was when Paul went to Damascus.

In the end-times small, rather fanatic, groups will arise, even as they are at the very moment. These are to be avoided. Just because we suspect that we are getting to the end-times, we are *not* to just pull up stakes, sell all our possessions, get dressed in white, and go into the mountains to await the arrival of the Lord. Such external reactions are of little worth. The reaction Our Lord wants is internal, a true conversion. Only those living in Judea and Jerusalem are told to flee when armies start to invade Jerusalem, no one else is. Also to start some sort of revolt is a rather useless thing. Others have done this in past ages but when Our Lord returns, *He* destroys His enemies. The saints come along, as spectators, for the view (Rev. 19:13–16). Isaiah 63:3 emphasizes that Our Lord does this *alone*. He needs no help. "Vengeance is mine," says the Lord (Deut. 32:35).

I would bring this book to a close on this final note of warning. St. Peter, in his second letter, Chapter 3, Verses 3 and 4, tells us quite clearly that in the latter days scoffers will appear and mock the prophetic word.

"Note this first of all: in the last days, mocking, sneering men who are ruled by their passions will arrive on the scene. They will ask: 'Where is that promised coming of His? Our forefathers have been laid to rest, but everything stays just as it was when the world was created.' "

We will meet with mockery and derision. But this is good. It is a fulfillment of Prophecy. For inevitably, inexorably, all the prophecies of Scripture will be fulfilled and the Prophetic WORD made manifest.

APPENDICES

APPENDICES

Selected Compilation of Texts

Preliminaries	Gospels	Rev.	Epistles	O.T.
Destruction of Temple	Mt. 24:1–2 Lk. 21:5–6			
Beginning of return of Jews to The Land	Mt. 24:15–21 Lk. 21:12			Hos. 3:4–5 Ezek. 36:24–28 Ezek. 37:1–14 Ezek. 39:25 Jer. 16:15
Hebrew religion again observed in The Land	Mt. 24:15–21			
Rebuilding of Temple	Mt. 24:15	11:1–2	2 Thess. 2:4	Mal. 3:1–2 Joel 1:14 Amos 9:11
Many false Messiahs	Mt. 24:5 Lk. 21:8			
Wars and rumors of wars, insurrections, famine, etc.	Lk. 21:9 Mt. 24:6			
Apostasy	Lk. 18:8	12:4	2 Thess. 2:3–4	
Peace and security (Normal times)	Mt. 24:45–51 Mk. 13:34–37		1 Thess. 5:3 2 Pt. 3:4–5 Jude 17	
As it was in the days of Noah	Mt. 24:36–41			Gen. 6:1–13
As it was in the days of Lot	Lk. 17:26–30		Rom. 1:21–28	Gen. 18:20 Ezek. 16:44–50
10 nation confederation ready		13:1–10		Dan. 2:31–45 Dan. 7:19–27 Dan. 8:9–25
Russia ready and willing				Ezek. 38 & 39 Joel 2
Prophecies become clear			1 Thess. 5:4 Heb. 10:25	Dan. 12:4 Dan. 12:9
Anti-Christ around but not yet recognized			2 Thess. 2:3–4 2 Thess. 2:8	

Great Sign No. 1	Gospels	Rev.	Epistles	O.T.
The Rapture	Lk. 17:26–36 Lk. 21:35–36 Lk. 21:28 Mt. 25:1–30	12:1–5 3:10	1 Thess. 4:13–18 1 Thess. 5:4–11 1 Cor. 15:51–58 2 Thess. 2:1–3; 2:7–8 Eph. 4:30 Tit. 2:13–15	
The Rapture— where and when	Lk. 17:34–36 Mt. 24:36		1 Thess. 5:1–2	

Redemption	Gospels	Rev.	Epistles	O.T.
Seal 1—White Horse Imperialism		6:2		
Seal 2—Red Horse Wars		6:3–4		
Seal 3—Black Horse Inflation—Famine		6:5–6		
Seal 4—Green (Pale) Horse Death, Plagues		6:7–8		
Seal 5—Martyrs	Mt. 10:17 Mt. 24:9–10 Lk. 21:12 Mk. 13:9–13	6:9–11 12:6–17 20:4		
Seal 6— Gog and Magog		6:12–17		Ezek. 38 & 39 Joel 2:1–27
Seal 7—*Pause* Revival and return of Jews	Mt. 24:14	14:6 14:8–9		Joel 2:28 Ezek. 31:14 Ezek. 39:25–29
Firm Covenant (to be broken)	Mt. 24:15–16 Mk. 13:14	13:15	2 Thess. 2:3–4	Dan. 9:27 Dan. 11:31 Dan. 7:25–26

Great Sign No. 2	Gospels	Rev.	Epistles	O.T.
Plague 1		8:7 16:2		
Plague 2		8:8 16:3		
Plague 3		8:10 16:4		
Plague 4		8:12 16:8		Joel 2:31

APPENDICES171

Great Sign No. 2	Gospels	Rev.	Epistles	O.T.
Plague 5		9:1 15:10		
"Jacob's Troubles"	Mt. 24:15–25 Lk. 21:20–24 Mk. 13:14–20	11:2–3 13:14–17		Dan. 11:31 Jer. 30:7–11
Enoch and Elijah	Mt. 17:11	11:3–13		Sirach 44:16; 48:10 Mal. 4:5–6 Isaiah 19 & 11:15
Plague 6—War— up to Armageddon	Mt. 24:21–22	9:12–20 16:12–16 11:18		Dan. 7:25
The Second Coming	Mt. 26:64 Mt. 24:26–31 Lk. 21:25–33 Mt. 25:31–46	11:14–19 16:17–21 19:11–20	1 Pt. 4:13 2 Pt. 3:10 Jude, 14–15	Joel 4:9–16 Job 38:22 Isaiah 24:20; 11:1–5 Zech. 12:10–14 Zech. 13:8 Zech. 14:1–15

APPENDIX II

Order of Events at the
Time of the Rapture

(a) Apostasy   2 Thess. 2:3   Rev. 12:4
(b) Rapture   2 Thess. 2:7   Rev. 12:5
(c) Anti-Christ   2 Thess. 2:8   Rev. 12:6–13
    appears in true colors

APPENDIX III

The Differences between the Rapture and the Second Coming

	The Rapture	The Coming
Who:	Those in Sanctifying Grace are taken up; others remain on earth. Eph. 4:30 1 Thess. 5:9 Titus 2:13 Heb. 9:28 Titus 3:7 Lk. 21:36 1 Cor. 15:58	The good remain on earth; the evil are slain and judged. Rev. 19:21 Rev. 20:11
What:	Christ's followers get glorified, rise up into clouds to meet Him, for the marriage feast of the Lamb. Rev. 19:7–9 1 Cor. 15:51–53 1 Thess. 4:15–18 Mt. 25:1–13	Christ comes down to earth accompanied by His saints to destroy those who are destroying the earth. Mt. 26:64 Jude 14 Rev. 19:12–20 Mal. 3:1–5 Rev. 11:18 2 Thess. 2:8
When:	We know not the day nor the hour. Mt. 24:36 Lk. 17:35 1 Thess. 5:1–6	3½ years after abomination of desolation, Dan. 12:11. 7 years after "The Treaty" is signed, Dan. 9:27. At Armageddon, the world's armies are lined up to oppose Christ. Rev. 11:18 Ps. 2:1–12
Where:	From all over the earth, to where Christ happens to be then, in the heavens. Mt. 24:26–28 Lk. 17:37	At Armageddon and nearby. Zech. 14:1–5
Why:	To preserve the good from the wrath to come. 1 Thess. 5:9–10	To destroy those who are destroying the earth. Rev. 11:18

	The Rapture	The Coming
Numbers included:	About one-half of those believing in God. Mt. 25:1–13 Lk. 17:34–36	An analysis of the seal judgments and plagues in Revelation indicates one-fourth of those left after the Rapture will be alive at the time of Armageddon. What percentage survives and enters the kingdom is not specified. Of the Jews, one-third of those around after the Russian debacle will enter the kingdom. Zech. 13:8–9
How:	At Christ's command, trumpet sounds, and archangel summons. 1 Thess. 4:16–17 1 Cor. 15:51–52	Christ, accompanied by His saints, strikes the nations. Rev. 19:15 Zech. 14:12–14 Rev. 19:21
Environment:	Peace and security, normal times. 1 Thess. 5:3 Lk. 17:26–31 Mt. 24:37–41	Earth ravaged by plagues, fiercest war of all history raging. Rev. 9:13–17 Rev. 16:12–21

The two events are nowhere mentioned as occurring together. If they were only minutes apart, all the good would be removed and glorified, all the evil destroyed and no one left to repopulate the kingdom. Time is needed between the two events for conversions: to faith and to good living.

APPENDIX IV

The Differences between the
Russian Invasion (Gog and Magog)
and Armageddon

	Russian Invasion	Armageddon
Partici- pants for:	Gog and country of Magog; prince of Rosh; Meshech; Tubal. Also Persia; Cush; Put; Gomer; Beth-togarmah—Ezek. 38:1–6. Gog is from "the recesses of the north," i.e., the farthest north—Ezek. 38:6; 38:15; 39:2.	The kings of the east—Rev. 17:12; beast, with *all* the kings of the earth and their armies—Rev. 19:19; Rev. 16:14; also Rev. 17:14; Dan. 11:40; *king of south* = Egypt and her allies; *king of north* (as opposed to *far* north) = Anti-Christ.
Against:	Israel—Ezek. 38:9. Sheba; Dedan; Tarshish and the young lions—Ezek. 38:13.	Israel—at least Jerusalem, Mt. Zion, the Temple—Rev. 14:1; 11:2; Joel 4:16. God—Ps. 2:2.
Purpose:	To plunder (Israel) for loot: gold, silver, cattle, unlimited spoil—Ezek. 38:12–13.	*Beginning:* king of south (Egypt) fights king of north (Anti-Christ)—Dan. 11:40; Jer. 46:7–10. *Middle:* kings of east come in—Rev. 16:12. *End:* kings of earth plotting against Yahweh and His Anointed—Psalms 2:1–9; Rev. 16:14; 12:12; Zech. 14:4; Acts 1:9–12. To destroy Jews, Israel totally.
of Satan:		Hatred of Christ.

	Russian Invasion	Armageddon
of God:	To display God's holiness to the nations; to serve as a last warning before Armageddon; the holocaust which occurs will be, clearly and definitively, from God; Russia will be converted; *God* will bring back the Jewish captives; *God* will pour out His spirit upon Israel—Ezek. 38 and 39; Joel 3:1–2; Jer. 16:14.	The time of God's wrath; the dead will be judged; the saints rewarded. *All* nations will be gathered to do battle; the time of judgment; the conversion of Jews to Christ—Rev. 11:18; Is. 34:2; Joel 4:2; Zech. 14:2; Zeph. 3:8; 3:1–2; Zech. 12:9.
Disposal of participants:	Gog and his horde buried in valley of Abarim—Ezek. 39:11. Also, the northern invader will be driven far from Israel, into a desolate land. Also God will send fire upon Magog, the coastlands, the islands—Ezek. 39:6.	*Rome* is destroyed in a single day—Rev. 18:8. *The armies* all destroyed by the sword of the rider (Christ)—Rev. 19:21. *Anti-Christ* and *Anti-Pope* are taken prisoner and thrown in lake of burning sulphur—Rev. 19:20. *Satan* is overcome by Michael and chained up for 1000 years—Rev. 20:3. *Survivors* are sent to the nation to proclaim God's glory—Is. 66:19.

Please Note: The Gog and Magog of Rev. 20:8 are not the same entities with which we have been dealing. Gog and Magog #2 are followed by a new Heaven and a new earth. Gog and Magog #1 are followed by 7 years of cleaning up. Also the second time around everything is destroyed by *fire* and Satan is thrown into the lake of fire forever and ever.

APPENDIX V
The Reasons for the Timing

The "latter days," "day of the Lord," "great tribulation" refer to one period, or parts of it that comprise 3 sections of approximately 3½ years each. Sometimes they are referred to as "time and times and half a time," or "1260 days" or "42 months." They are frequently thought to be simultaneous, yet Scripture tells us they are consecutive times.

A brief glance shows that the trumpet judgments and bowl judgments of Revelation are identical, repetitions of each other and that the 7 Seal judgments come before them. The bowl and trumpet judgments are 7 consecutive plagues, listed in order, and the duration of some of them is accurately specified. The 7 Seal judgments are essentially events that overlap each other, and their total time is specified.

(a) The 7 Seal judgments come *before* the trumpet and bowl judgments.

Rev. 7:2–3: "Hurt not the earth till the servants are sealed." So the plagues are held off for the time being. Rev. 8:3: The 7th Seal is opened, followed by silence for one half hour. There is a short gap, an interval yet before the plagues start. Rev. 8:7: Then the first trumpet sounds and the plagues begin.

(b) The Seal judgments take *3½ years*.

Rev. 6:9–11: The martyrs of this period are seen waiting impatiently under the altar, and being told to wait a while, till their number is complete. Rev. 13:5: Power is given to the beast (Anti-Christ) for 42 months. Rev. 13:7: Power to make war against the saints and to conquer them, power over every race, people, etc., for 42 months. After that, the persecution ends, but the international wars go on.

The first 5 Seal judgments consist of imperialism, war, famine, death, and persecution; while Anti-Christ establishes his power.

The 6th Seal judgment is relatively brief, and the 7th one brief but not specified. The total time allotted, then, is 3½ years plus possibly a short interval, corresponding to the half

177

hour of silence. Then Anti-Christ's reign is shaken by the 7 last plagues, the trumpet and bowl judgments.

(c)   The 6th Seal judgment corresponds to the war of Gog and Magog.

Rev. 6:12 describes parts of this 6th Seal judgment as a huge earthquake, the sun black as sackcloth, the moon like blood, and the stars falling from heaven. Joel 2:10; 2:31: describes the same darkening of the sun and the moon turning to blood and earthquakes occurring at the destruction of the *northern* enemy (Joel 2:20). This is the northern enemy described in Ezekiel 38 and 39 where the destruction is given in greater detail. Joel 2:28 tells us of the pouring out of the Spirit on all flesh after this event, but *before* the "day of the Lord" which is described in the 3rd chapter of Joel, at the end of which *all* (Joel 3:2 or 4:2) nations are gathered into the Valley of Jehosaphat, for the battle of Armageddon. Then, too, the sun and moon are darkened again, with a second fierce earthquake and hail (Joel 4:15–16). This is described also in Rev. 11:19 (seventh trumpet) and Rev. 16:18–20 (seventh bowl).

Therefore—

The 6th Seal judgment is the vast earthquake, hail, etc., that wipes out the "northern enemy" and his numerous allies and those living "undisturbed in the islands" (Ezek. 39:6). This may be a separate war, or just one phase or campaign in Anti-Christ's wars. It will be followed by mass conversions to God, by Jews and Gentiles alike (Joel 3:1). But the "day of the Lord" corresponds to the 7 bowl and 7 trumpet plagues, which culminate in the battle of Armageddon where the assembled armies of the world are destroyed. Mt. 13:42; Rev. 11:18–19.

(d)   Dan. 9:24; Lev. 25:8: a "seven of years."

Dan. 9:27: He (the prince of the people that destroyed the temple) shall confirm the covenant for one week, and in the middle of the week the sacrifice shall fail, and there shall be in the temple the abomination of desolation—even to the end. Dan. 11:31; 12:11; 7:25; 8:14; 8:17; Mt. 24:15; Rev. 13:15.

Therefore—

There is a 7 year period when Anti-Christ makes a firm covenant with Israel. Approximately in the middle of this period, he ends the sacrifice and sets up the "abomination of desolation," probably his talking statue (if not himself personally for a while). According to Mt. 24:16 those in Judea know when that abomination of desolation occurs, immediately.

Between the Covenant and the end is 7 years.

After the destruction of Gog, there are *at least* 7 years (Ezek. 39:9) to clean up the debris. There may be more time.

A quite probable interpretation: After Gog's destruction, Anti-Christ offers a 7 year defense treaty to Israel. Since the neighboring countries are hostile and Israel's only allies (Saba, Dedan, young lions of Tarshish) (Ezek. 38:13) are distant, and perhaps weakened (Ezek. 39:6, fire on the islands), they accept. Anti-Christ is now the protector of Israel, instead of God, and he takes over, and gets himself worshipped in the Temple. The total time between Gog's destruction and the end may be more than 7 years, because there can be an interval between Gog's destruction and the Treaty. (Rev. 8:1: the 7th Seal—silence—for a half hour or so—and then the trumpet and bowl judgments begin.) After the 6th Seal, 7 years, possibly plus some more, to the end. During this time, the trumpet and bowl judgments have to occur.

(e) During the final 3½ years the Temple is trodden underfoot by the Gentiles for 42 months (Rev. 11:2) and then comes the end (Rev. 11:15).

Therefore—

The 6th trumpet (Rev. 9:13) takes almost 3½ years alone. This corresponds to the second half of Daniel's last week. Now trumpet 5 alone takes 5 months. So the first 5 trumpets seem to correspond to the first half of Daniel's week, since they come *after* the 7th Seal is opened (Rev. 8:2) and *before* trumpet #6 which corresponds to most of Daniel's 2nd half week.

Therefore—

Trumpets 6 and 7 . . . take . . .   3½ years

. . . .

Trumpets 1 through 7, inclusive =   7   years
Seals   = 3½ years
                        Total = 10½ years
                        (possibly a little more)

Therefore—

Around 10½ years before the Second Coming Anti-Christ reveals his true nature, and the wars and the persecutions begin, right after the Rapture.